The aficionado's guidebook to saltwater fishing.
— Jay Dail, Coastal Conservation Association

The Southern Surfcaster ranks high among the best
publications I've seen devoted to casting baits and lures
into the surf.
—Tom Higgins, *Charlotte Observer*

Cameron Wright is truly a master of his genre.
—Gregg Kielma, ESPN

THE SOUTHERN SURFCASTER

SALTWATER STRATEGIES FOR THE CAROLINA BEACHES & BEYOND

S. CAMERON WRIGHT

Charleston   London

THE
History
PRESS

Published by The History Press
Charleston, SC 29403
www.historypress.net

Unless otherwise noted, images are courtesy of Sea Striker International, Steve
Luther and Cameron Wright.

First published 2012

Manufactured in the United States

ISBN 978.1.60949.677.7

Library of Congress CIP data applied for.

Notice: The information in this book is true and complete to the best of our
knowledge. It is offered without guarantee on the part of the author or The
History Press. The author and The History Press disclaim all liability in
connection with the use of this book.

This book is dedicated to my wife, Liz, my three wonderful sons, Zach, Connor and Vance, and my loving parents, Hollis and Shirley Wright.

Contents

Preface

History confirms the bountiful harvest our oceans do yield. Those who came before us and those who shall succeed will undoubtedly partake in her abundance. Whether you are new to the sport or are a seasoned veteran, becoming a proficient angler requires considerable effort and the mastering of many skills. Accept and take comfort in the understanding that this sport requires your serving an apprenticeship. Unfortunately, there are no shortcuts, nor are there any Cliff Notes to hasten the learning curve. This book will guide you through the essential skills and knowledge required to catch fish from the beach. Transforming from a novice fisherman into a veteran angler can only be achieved with time spent honing your skills. Fishing veterans should be prepared to help teach the newbies as they venture into the sport. I have spent countless hours helping the new guys rig and bait up while everyone else is casting away.

Experience will translate into more bountiful quarries as you navigate the stages on the path to edification in becoming a seasoned angler. After all, 10 percent of the fishermen catch 90 percent of the fish!

This book is intended to educate the novice, as well as refine some new techniques for the experienced angler. You will gain a solid understanding of the various components involved with the sport. Surf fishing is about relaxing with friends and enjoying an occasional gourmet meal for saltwater anglers. Our sport provides and maintains thousands of jobs in coastal and inland communities. Commercial fishing accounts for nearly ninety million tons of fish captured per year worldwide. The primary species harvested for commercial use include cod, herring, salmon, shrimp, anchovy and tuna. The top-producing commercial fishing countries are China, Japan and Russia. It is estimated that seafood generates approximately 20 percent of the world's sustenance.

Sport fishing generates hundreds of millions of dollars annually to the economy. Penned within these pages are four decades of invaluable knowledge and time-tested experience that will elevate your angling skills to the next level and beyond. This book is my compilation of material that has been passed down from generations to be your personal guide on your journey to the pinnacle of surf fishing, designed with essential and indispensable experience that has taken nearly half a century to compile.

Surf fishing is a specialized form of fishing that demands advanced preparation and having proper equipment. The tackle used by surf anglers encompasses a variety of specialized gear. Tackle selection is determined by which species of fish you are targeting and the conditions in which you are fishing. Having the appropriate gear for any variety of conditions that may arise during a given day is paramount. Fishing from the surf requires more patience and ability than any other method of angling. Learning to become a confident surf angler requires mastering the basic essentials while exerting the utmost patience.

Surf fishing is my passion, which has enabled me to create special memories that are both enduring and everlasting. In addition to serving as your personal guidebook, this book will allow you to become enlightened with some pointed insight into our rich southern traditions and nuances. I have taken the liberty to document several topics of historical significance that have helped define our region's characteristics. It is my intention that you will adopt some of the vernacular semantics that distinguish our culture from all others.

Acknowledgements

This book would not have happened without the countless hours of editorial assistance and hard work of my very good friend Steve Luther. Special thanks to my lifelong friends and fishing buddies Skip Robinson and Bill Powers. Thanks also go to:

George Poveromo
Tom Higgins, *Charlotte Observer*
ESPN Gregg Kielma
Coastal Conservation Association, Jay Dail
South Carolina Natural Resources, Marine Resources Division
North Carolina Division of Marine Fisheries
North Carolina State University
Montreat College Library
Harry Nilsson, author, *The Little Red Book of Fishing Knots*
Park Road Books, Charlotte, North Carolina
United States Coast Guard Auxiliary
Park Crossing Surf Casting Club

International Game Fish Association (IGFA), Florida
Mark Suba, Sea Striker International, Morehead City, North Carolina
Mr. Duane Raver for sharing his wonderful fish illustrations.
Saltwater Sportsman Magazine
Peter Meyer, Avian-Cetacean Press
Ray Craven
Joe Harris
Robert Aliota
Michael McGill
Andy Wright
Greg Wright
Jeff Wright

Introduction

There are few absolutes in the sport of surf fishing. Whether you are new to the sport or are a seasoned veteran, becoming a proficient angler takes considerable effort and the mastering of many skills. *The Southern Surfcaster* will increase your knowledge of fishing and help you develop into a more confident saltwater fisherman by exploring creative techniques and the latest strategies that have transformed the sport over the last decade. Many of the old-school methods of fishing have been updated for modern practicality. *The Southern Surfcaster* will change the way you think and what you thought you knew about saltwater fishing. The application of appropriate fishing components is explained in complete detail. Knowing which rigs and tackle to deploy under any circumstance is vital to successful inshore fishing. Presentation of the correct bait and lures used to catch your quarry is covered step by step. Understanding the dynamics of weather, beach and surf conditions is key to a trouble-free trip. The coastal region of North and South Carolina is the primary venue that is discussed. Learn where, when and how to maximize your results that will yield many successful fishing excursions. Familiarization with the types of fish indigenous to our waters is very important. Twenty of the most popular species of fish are summarized and explained in full detail within this book. Each of the species discussed is accompanied by a detailed illustration for proper identification. My journey on the path to fishing edification has taken me around the world. An intriguing compilation of some of my fishing excursion highlights in Africa,

Australia and South America are shared as well. There are certain customs and proper etiquette that are recommended when interacting with the locals around our coastal villages and towns. Explore some of the rich heritage that has helped define the southern Atlantic as the country's most historic seaboard.

Chapter 1

Spikes in the Sand
Put Fish in Your Hands

EDIFICATION AT LAST

Many have asked when a fisherman is no longer considered a novice to the sport. This question has several answers, of which most are correct. Sport fishing has basically four levels of apprenticeship. They are in this order: catching *any* Fish, catching *many* fish, catching the *biggest* fish and catching the *best* fish (I am not quoting Dr. Seuss). The four stages are very elementary in their explanation and are quite accurate. Passing from one stage to the next is rewarding within itself. The four levels of refinement are true. The "newbie" will be ecstatic to catch anything that swims. Not long after, a season or two, he will want to prove his salt by catching a large enough haul to feed the family. Several seasons will pass again, as will his desire for the masses. Alas, he wants the big one; no longer will the fish smaller in stature be suitable. He wants the citation-trophy fish. The advanced stage seems to keep one's attention far longer than the previous two stages of any fish and many fish. When the angler has arrived at this level, he is able to pursue his targeted species. Ascending to this graduate level of the sport empowers him with knowledge. He is nearly at the pinnacle of the sport. He is comfortable as to where to locate his quarry. He knows which rig to deploy under what conditions. He is readily able to work his offering in such a way as to land his target species more often than not using proven experience and technique. When he is able to consistently pursue and catch targeted species of fish, he has arrived. Being considered a pro is more than being able to catch fish in a tournament. It comes with a responsibility to the sport and the environment. Earning this status requires being a steward of the ocean and a teacher to others. When you arrive at this status, others will take note of your mannerisms and confidence and the way in which you handle yourself on the beach. Becoming a proficient angler will require you having paid your dues of time spent in the surf. Fellow anglers confess that having earned this confidence is empowering. I hold the opinion that you do not have to prove your salt by chasing only large fish. I am usually more content pursuing a mixed bag. Keep in mind that when you are fishing, you have nothing to prove to anyone. Do not become overly obsessed to the point that you become disappointed if you do not land a trophy fish every time out. Don't concern yourself with anything other than enjoying yourself while fishing in the surf. From time to time, there will be the occasion when the fish are just not hitting. This is why the sport is called "fishing," not "catching." Do not assume that you are going to catch a bounty of fish on each and every excursion. Not only will this false hope set you up for disappointment, but it can also negatively predispose your future outings.

The ancient practice of fishing dates back to the Paleolithic period nearly forty thousand years ago. Gathering fish for sustenance during Paleolithic times was accomplished by the use of harpoons and barbed spears. Roman mosaics depict spear fishing from small boats along the Mediterranean, while the Greeks relied more on fishing with seines. The Chinese would bait the water with grains of rice and use drift nets crafted from silk to fish. Fishing evolved into a more modern approach in Scandinavia when the Norwegians introduced the first barbed metal hook in the twelfth century. Fishing for cod, one of the oldest traded commodities in the world, originated during the Viking period. The residents of Scotland engaged in coastal fishing with the use of a gorge hook and line tackle. Fishing continued to gain momentum throughout Europe in the late fifteenth century along the coastline of the British Isles with the advent of rudimentary rods and reels. The first record of coastal fishing using a hook and line in the Carolinas was attributed to the Scotch-Irish in the pre-colonial period. As evidence to its popularity, fishing from the shore was common among both Union and Confederate soldiers during the War Between the States.

The popularity of surf fishing as we know it today coincided with the development of technology and equipment. The first commercially available fishing rods that were produced in North America were manufactured by Hiram Leonard. His revolutionary fishing rods were hexagonal in diameter and were constructed with split and glued bamboo. Leonard's fishing rods were fashioned with four to six eyelets that were composed of wire rings. The original mechanical fishing reels were constructed of a wooden spool with a crude metal clamp ring that was used as a clutch. Fishing line crafted from horsehair was replaced by that made of silk, which was heavy enough for casting. Nylon monofilament fishing line was developed and introduced in the late 1930s.

Participation in the sport expanded greatly in the 1950s along the coast of both North and South Carolina. Family beach vacations gained tremendous popularity after the conclusion of World War II. Our soldiers were eager to recreate at the seashore. The majority of these soldiers had never seen the coast prior to their disembarkation to Europe and the Pacific to serve overseas. The rapid abundance and availability of new automobiles after the war sent vacationers to the coast in great numbers. The continued popularity of beach vacations has been the lifeblood of surf fishing along the Carolina coast.

As the sport of saltwater fishing transformed, the industry has become a billion-dollar recreation that continues to strengthen in popularity. During the last two decades, we have seen the sport evolve with corporate sponsorships, million-dollar-purse fishing tournaments and syndicated television productions.

SALTWATER FISHING VERSUS FRESHWATER FISHING

I am often asked why saltwater fishing is more difficult to master than fishing in fresh water. It is true that fishing in lakes, streams and rivers is less complicated than fishing in the ocean. Several elements that support this comparison are obvious. Most freshwater venues will afford you easy access from the bank or dock to the water. By easy access, I refer to being able to have a solid or well-suited position from which to operate. Usually, these positions will afford you some elevation from which to cast. Standing on the open beach, you will have to deal with the sand and incoming waves. Working from a soft, sandy beach in which your feet sink is physically demanding over several hours and requires some stamina. Fishing from the surf offers very little structure for the angler on the beach or for the fish in the water. For those anglers who want the best of both worlds, try the pier, which is less challenging both physically and technically.

Fishing in freshwater venues provides a stable platform from which to operate. Fishing at the water's edge on a lake or river provides solid footing for the angler. Many lake anglers will have access to a dock or an elevated riverbank. Not worrying about your feet and gear sinking into the soft sand or having your gear overrun with waves is a luxury. The presence of natural structures such as brush or felled trees offers an abundance of shade for fish to take refuge from the sun. Fishing from the surf affords very little structure, if any, for protection. Take advantage of any floating debris or submerged pilings. Let us not take for granted the daunting task of staring upon the vast open ocean with no obvious presence of fish. Our brethren who fish offshore have the distinct advantage of traveling great distances to locate favorable fishing grounds. In addition to mobility, they have the prime advantage of being fully equipped with all the modern weaponry of a fully outfitted sport-fishing vessel. We, the purists, meticulously choose a location and patiently await our quarry.

TACKLE REQUIREMENTS

Very few fishermen are satisfied with the first outfit they purchase as a novice in the sport. This is especially true for surf anglers. You can become outfitted with a very basic rod, reel and tackle for about $100. If you fish only once or twice each year, then this gear will probably be satisfactory. I am frequently asked why it is recommended that surf fishermen have at least two complete rod and reel combinations. The primary reason is that when you go on an outing, you have no way of knowing what type of fish is going to strike! Therefore, if you are set up with light-action tackle and you get into large drum or blues, it is very probable that your equipment will not survive the encounter. On the other hand, if you are using heavier surf tackle, chances are that you will not feel the strike and thus lose your bait and your smaller species of fish. With some experience, we are able to regulate or predetermine which type or family of fishes we attract. We will not cast out a drum rig on light tackle. Nor do we typically cast an artificial lure out with a Hatteras Heaver!

Being a sentimental guy, I find it difficult to relinquish any of my retired gear. To this day, I still have my first Sears Roebuck fishing rod that my parents bought me as a boy, and I proudly display it on the wall in my library. I have made the attempt on more than one occasion to calculate my accumulated investment in fishing tackle over the years. My expenditures surpassed what I spent on my first and second automobiles and a semester of college combined! I have chosen never to reveal most of my tackle acquisitions with my bride. I am fearful that this disclosure would empower my wife's pursuit of her own expensive shopping habits.

Choosing the appropriate tackle for the right conditions is paramount. I almost always use my first small catch of the day as bait for one of my larger outfits. Having my "big rig" baited in the surf has afforded me plenty of action when the smaller to medium fish are not active.

The term "balanced tackle" does not refer to the weighted dynamic or static balance of your gear. Rather, it refers to the relationship between your rod, reels, line and rigs. Make certain when you assemble to purchase your rod, reels and line that you properly select gear that is reasonable proportionate to the matching components. Having well-balanced outfits will help ensure effective casting and proper retrieval. If the weight is not properly balanced between your components, the distance and accuracy will suffer. Balance is equally as critical between the line and rig/lure weight.

One of the most important habits that you must develop is maintaining your gear. Always, without failure, rinse all of your tackle with *fresh water* after each day of use! This must be done every time. Failing to do so even once can result in irreparable damage to your equipment. The salt air and especially the salt water will corrode your gear in a few days' time. When you reel in your rig, the water that comes off your line covers everything. Your reels are especially susceptible to corrosion. The first thing you will do upon returning from the beach (not just at the end of the trip) is to rinse thoroughly every rod and reel. I prefer a garden hose without the spray attachment. The salt water that collects on your gear is residual; it will rinse off with normal garden hose pressure. Using a spray attachment can force salt water into the interior of your reel. I do not suggest that you submerge your reel under water. This, too, allows water to work its way into the interior components of your reel. Tighten down the drag to minimize water intrusion. Even the most expensive, high-quality reels are not intended to have the inner mechanisms exposed to water.

Chapter 2

Fishing Rods and Reels

SPINNING RODS

Spinning rods are constructed from fiberglass or graphite affixed with a cork or foam-like PVC handle. Surf spinning rods usually range from seven and a half to twelve feet in length. The typical spinning rod usually is outfitted with six to ten large diameter guides arranged along the underside of the rod to keep the line away from the rod blank. The guides decrease in size from the handle to the tip. The large gathering guide nearest the reel will prevent your line from slapping against the blank during a cast. Unlike conventional reels, spinning reels hang beneath the rod instead of on top like bait-casting rods. The reel is held in place by a sliding lock mechanism that is screwed onto the reel seat. Most spinning rods over eight feet in length are two-piece models for ease of transportation and stowage. Spinning gear is used more often than conventional tackle for surf fishing. Unlike conventional rod and reel outfits, spinning combinations are easier to use and are less likely to foul than conventional bait-casting tackle.

CONVENTIONAL RODS

Commonly known as bait-casting rods, conventional rods are designed to hold a matching reel on the top of the rod, unlike the spinning reel, which hangs from the bottom of the reel seat. Effective use of conventional tackle

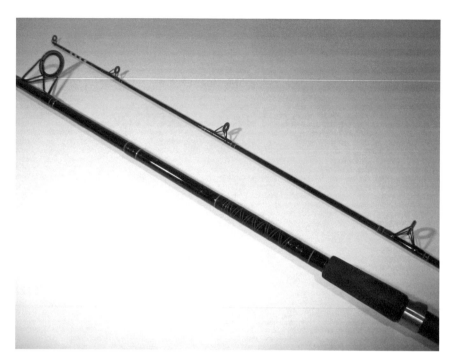

Spinning rod.

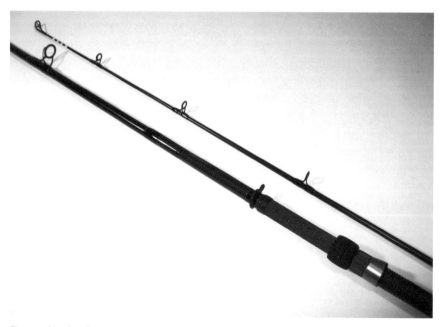

Conventional rod.

requires practice and careful "thumbing" of the line as it leaves the spool to prevent backlashing. Conventional tackle is preferred by anglers fishing with very heavy payloads of eight ounces or more and using twenty-five-pound-plus line. Bait-casting rods also utilize small-diameter eyelets. Most bait-casting rods are at least ten feet long and are constructed from a heavy blank. Conventional rods have more eyelets or guides than do their spin-casting cousins. The first guide is generally spaced thirty-three inches from the reel seat, with the other spaced along the blank closer in position as they reach the tip. The majority of heavy offshore equipment will be conventional tackle with short, stocky rods with heavy reels, spooled with eighty-pound-plus monofilament. These rods are also referred to as "boat rods."

THE AQUATIC GRIDIRON

In football, most quarterbacks are tall enough to survey down the field or to deliver a pass over the line of scrimmage. Your rod is the quarterback. The line of scrimmage you are trying to get past are the breakers. A quarterback who can't clear the line is usually not that effective. Sometimes you will need to be able to clear the breakers when you are attempting to cast over the rolling surf. Granted, casting beyond the breakers is not always the objective. Physics concludes that the longer your rod, the farther you will be able to cast. In football, quarterbacks do not like to get hit. Neither does your fishing rod. Never let your rigs or weights hit your rod blank, as this can greatly reduce its strength. This applies when you're casting and, more importantly, when you are transporting your gear. Do not walk to and from the beach with your rigs or lures improperly secured. They will become entangled with most everything that comes within reach. Proper rod selection is primarily dependent on the weight of the rig or lure and the distance in which you plan to cast. Longer rods will afford you greater casting distance with lighter-weight payloads. Conversely, shorter, stouter rods will afford you increased fighting leverage and greater casting accuracy.

ROD GUIDES/EYELETS

The function of your rod guides is twofold. First, properly placed rod guides will ensure that your load is distributed evenly over the entire length of your rod. Second, they keep your line free and clear of the blank during cast and retrieval. Always take care to ensure that your rod guides are well maintained. Pay attention to the guide frames and other metal components.

Use of a corrosion inhibitor is recommended on the guide feet. Avoid using aerosol-type lubricants; instead, try using a drip dispenser or can. Use your index finger to feel for nicks or abrasions that can damage or even cut your line. Pass a cotton ball through each eyelet to determine if you have any cracks or fissures that are not visible. If the eyelets "pick" any fiber, you will see where the problem is. Particular attention should be given to the rod tip. This is the eyelet on the very end of your rod that is the easiest to damage. A damaged rod tip will most certainly result in line failure. More eyelets mean improved weight and stress distribution throughout the parabolic arc. This equates to less potential rod failure and increased casting distance. Ceramic guides are much preferred over stainless steel. Ceramic guides allow for less friction and longer casts with less line fray. Never reel in your rig or lure to the point that the metal hardware comes into contact with the rod tip. The metal hardware can nick the ceramic tip, which can damage your line. Reeling in your rig or lure to the point that it bends your rod can cause the tip of your rod to break. Over time, your guides can become damaged, which can lead to line fatigue.

PARABOLIC ROD ACTION

This action refers to the responsiveness and flexibility of the rod when force is applied. Casting accuracy is governed by the action and speed at the tip of the rod.

Very fast action: Rod flex in the upper $1/4$ of the rod blank closest to the tip.
Fast action: Rod flex in the upper $1/3$ of the rod blank.
Moderate action: Rod flex near the middle $1/2$ of the rod blank.
Slow action: Rod flex in the lower $1/2$ of the rod blank closest to the reel.

Slow-action rods are better suited for casting lures due to overall flexibility of the entire rod. Fast-action rods are better suited for casting payloads such as heavily weighted rigs.

Weight and line ratings are usually located on each rod. These are OEM specifications that should be followed. Following the manufacturers' recommendations can prevent breakage.

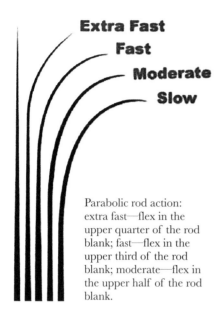

Parabolic rod action: extra fast—flex in the upper quarter of the rod blank; fast—flex in the upper third of the rod blank; moderate—flex in the upper half of the rod blank.

Action and taper refer to the way in which a rod bends. The tip of your rod determines the action and ultimately the casting accuracy. When quality rod blanks are manufactured, the wall thickness of the blank is kept uniform from the tip to the base. Surf fishing rods vary in how they are rated dependent on the method of fishing. Most spin-cast rods are rated extra fast to fast because this action generally provides increased sensitivity for rig casting and setting power.

Moderate and moderate-fast action rods will provide you with more casting distance. When fishing with artificial lures, consider a moderate- to slow-action rod so that you may feel and control the lure action and presentation. Normally, the size and weight of lure that you use will determine the action of the rod you should use. A longer, more parabolic rod allows you to generate greater tip speed, load your rod up and let fly your load.

There is no one fishing rod that will handle the full spectrum of fishing requirements. Surf anglers, in particular, usually have an arsenal of at least three rods when going out on an expedition. A slower-action rod generally is a less costly rod blank. The slower action affords the entire rod to bend under pressure. This action of rod is not well suited for casting heavy payloads. Moving up the scale to medium-action rods will afford you a more balanced action for broader fishing methods. The fast-action or taper rods will bend primarily in the upper portion of the blank. The extra-fast-action rod will provide you with more backbone toward the rod's lower portion.

CHOOSING THE CORRECT ROD

When choosing a fishing rod, you have to have a basic idea of what type of fishing you expect to do. Consider these basic criteria for types of fishing: heavy surfcasting with heavy weight, moderate surfcasting with mid-range weight or casting lighter artificial weight. We want to balance distance, power and accuracy. Consider the action that is right for your type of fishing. The slower the rod, the greater the bend from tip to base. The motion of this action is parabolic in that the rod bend is distributed evenly throughout the blank. The most popular surf rods for most anglers are seven to nine feet long. Larger rods, such as a Hatteras Heaver, are a bit overpowering for all but the most proficient anglers. Using a fast-action rod is designed and suited for casting heavy rigs of six to ten ounces. If your objective is to balance distance with moderate-weight rigs of three to five ounces, consider an eight-foot medium-action rod. Consider your rod material and guides. The guides keep your line evenly distributed along the rod and away from the blank, maximizing power and sensitivity while reducing friction. High-quality rods are constructed with high intermediate modulus (IM) graphite. The modulus rating refers to the amount of elasticity of the graphite. The higher the IM rating on your rod, the lighter the weight and the more sensitivity you get.

Manufacturer's Line Pound-Test Rating

Fishing rods are also classified by the optimal line rating as to the line weight the rod is designed to accommodate. Fishing line weight is rated in pounds of shearing force before the line breaks. When the line weight used significantly exceeds the rod's rating, the rod may break during the cast before full release. Conversely, if the line weight is greatly less than the rod's recommended rating, the line can break as the rod is loaded during cast.

Rig/Lure Weight Rating

Modern fishing rods are also rated as to the optimal weight of the rig or lure that the rod is designed to support. Universally, this rating is expressed in ounces. Greatly overloading the rod's weight rating can lead to rod failure when casting. Be cognizant to account for the extra weight of your bait when calculating your rod load.

Handles and Grips

Higher-end fishing rods use a low-density cork as the material for the handle. Cork is lightweight, durable and retains warmth more than synthetic materials such as high-density foam. Cork grips transmit rod vibrations better than any other material. This increased sensitivity affords the angler a better feel for strikes. Many rod grips are made with Hypalon or other synthetic, foam/rubber-like materials. Always make certain that your rod handle is washed clean with fresh, soapy water after each trip. The handle must be allowed to completely dry before storage to prevent mold and mildew. This applies for both fore and primary grips.

Reel Seats

The reel seat is the portion of the rod between the two handles that holds and seats your reel. The reel seat is usually constructed of graphite or reinforced plastic. Some manufacturers use aluminum as well. The reel seat is located well up the handle for optimum leverage. The majority of reel seats have a screw type of closure that cranks down on the reel feet to secure firmly in place. Make certain to always remove your reel and clean the reel seat and the threaded keyways as well. Polish dry and store your reels unattached.

ROD CLASSIFICATIONS/INSHORE AND SURF

ULTRA-LIGHT OUTFITS: Ultra-light gear is usually the last type of tackle that an angler will try. These rods start at eight feet long and can go up to twelve feet in length. The line rating is usually four to eight pounds. They have very slow action that enables the user to cast lightweight lures weighing less than one ounce great distances. These rods are very flexible and can really get a lightweight lure way out beyond the breakers. They provide the most fun when you hook up a fish. Be careful not to exceed the weight rating on these very temperamental outfits, as the rod tips will break if stressed beyond their rating.

MEDIUM/LIGHT OUTFITS: They are seven to nine feet in length, with a line rating of up to eight to twelve pounds. No shock leader is recommended, as the loss of feel would be compromised. Casting weight is three ounces or less in general. They are not capable of casting great distances, nor do they perform well in rough seas. These rods are well suited for the novice who is getting used to the concept of casting and retrieval, as they are easier to control. These outfits provide plenty of sport when fishing larger fish inshore.

MEDIUM OUTFITS: These are eight to ten and a half feet in length, with a line rating of between twelve and twenty pounds. Shock leader is optional but highly recommended. Casting weight is four to six ounces. Medium-action rods are the most popular rods on the beach. The impetus for selecting a medium-action rod is the compromise between casting distance and power. They afford the near perfect balance for overall surf-fishing requirements.

HEAVY OUTFITS: These are ten and a half to fourteen feet in length. The primary purpose of a longer/heavier rod is to deploy the heaviest of payloads into the surf and well beyond the breakers. These heavy outfits are well suited for use in the roughest of seas. More often than not, only well-seasoned anglers will use this category of tackle due to the complexities of their use. These rods are commonly referred to as Hatteras Heavers, due in part to the extreme fishing requirements along the Outer Banks of North Carolina. The line rating is twenty-five pounds and greater, with weights of up to ten ounces. Always use a shock leader when casting out more than six ounces of weight. Remember to take into account the weight of your baited rig or lure, in addition to your sinker, when calculating your load capacity.

SALTWATER FLY RODS

Fly rods are thin, flexible rods designed to cast very little weight. They usually have an artificial fly consisting of a hook affixed with feathers or lightweight balsa wood. Fly rods are constructed from man-made composites, such as fiberglass or carbon/graphite. Instead of a weighted rig or lure, a fly-fishing rod uses the weight of the special fly line for casting. These long and lightweight rods are slow to moderate in action and afford the casting of the very lightest and smallest fly. When fly-casting weighted flies, be careful not to hit the rod blank with the weighted fly. This can damage the rod blank and greatly reduce performance. Fly-fishing is fatiguing and requires much practice and patience. I rely on Jessie Brown's Outdoors in Charlotte for advice and equipment.

CARE AND HANDLING OF RODS

Take extreme care when transporting your rod. Deep scratches and nicks will greatly reduce its strength. Completely disassemble your rods before transporting. Remove any dirt, sand or other debris from the male ferrule before inserting it into the female ferrule section. Slowly twist and push the rod sections until the guides are properly aligned.

Ferrule Freeze

The ferrule union or joint is the point at which your rod is assembled into one piece. Ferrule freeze is the common problem of having difficulty separating or breaking down the two ends of your rod. The ferrule joint is designed to keep your eyelets aligned and your rod ends securely seated during use. The reason for this is that saltwater, sand and calcium residue get into or onto the connection points where your rod ends join. It has happened to all of us—we pull and we twist trying to break down our rods. I have seen many novices use their eyelets or guides for leverage while trying to separate their gear. Solution: use a small piece of emery cloth, three by three inches, tightly rolled into the shape of a pencil. Firmly, holding onto one end of your cloth, insert it into the female end of your rod. Make three complete rotations counterclockwise to dislodge any hardened buildup. Pointing your rod downward, remove your cloth and tap the open end lightly. Using Ivory soap, make several passes, rubbing the male end with your soap. This will help ensure that your two ends remain together until you require for easy separation.

Remove any sand, dirt or other debris from the ferrule section prior to inserting it into the female ferrule section. Slowly twist and push the rod sections together until the guides are properly aligned. Remember, *never* use your guides/eyelets for leverage when turning. Periodically apply a thin film of soap or wax to the male ferrule section. This will allow your rod's sections to seat securely, which prevents them from separating during use.

Eyelets need protection from damage during storage and transport. To avoid mildew, never store your rod away until it is very clean and completely dry. Make certain that your entire rod is free of sand, fish blood and saltwater residue. When storing your rods, ensure that the tips are never bent. This will keep them true and straight.

INDUSTRIAL ROD TRANSPORT CASE

Since I do not reside at the beach, I am relegated to transporting my gear to and from the coast. Trying to transport an eleven- or twelve-foot fishing rod is no easy task, and neither is trying to store it at home if your spouse does not share your love for fishing. I prefer two-piece rods that I can fit into my special rod carrier. The vast majority of fishermen will not be able to detect a difference in performance between a one-piece or two-piece rod. I have never been hindered by the loss of sensitivity of using a two-piece rod. There are some rods on the market that break down into three pieces. I prefer not to use these due to the awkwardness of assembly and handling.

High-quality one-piece fishing rods are very expensive. More rods get damaged during transport to and from the beach than during actual fishing. This is preventable if you properly protect your investment. The best way to ensure that your rods do not get broken is to carry them in a protective case. You can make your own with these materials from your local plumbing supply store:

- One piece ten-inch diameter PVC pipe, one-quarter-inch wall thickness, seven feet long
- One heavy-duty exterior end cap
- One screw-on cap sold as a clean-out plug

ROD ID

I strongly suggest that every fisherman do the following: Go to your local hardware store and purchase a single roll of colored electrical tape. Choose any bright color that you like. (I use bright yellow.) Pull off one inch of tape. Cut the tape long ways into quarter-inch pieces. Between your rod tip and the first eyelet, wrap around your rod. Spread these four strips out with one inch in between each band. This is done for two reasons: 1) you will be able to detect movement (strikes) much easier, even from a distance; and 2) all of your rods will be "coded" with the same color and pattern so that you will be able to notice if your colors are being transported by someone other than the rightful owner.

Safe Usage and Care and Handling

If your rig becomes snagged, point your rod directly at the rig and pull back with a slow rocking motion. This puts stress on the line rather than your rod. This will ensure that you do not break your rod on a snag. Your rod will fail if you bend it in an arc that is tighter than its design will allow.

Do not place your hand on the rod blank above the handle while fighting or attempting to land a fish. This will put excessive pressure at the single point where your hand is placed rather than allowing the rod to distribute the pressure exerted over the entire length of the blank. This is called "high sticking" and can break your rod. Use caution when fishing with graphite rods during an electrical storm. Graphite rod blanks contain carbon fibers that are excellent conductors of electricity.

Fishing Reels

The primary function of any fishing reel is to keep your line evenly spooled and ready to cast. Both conventional and spinning reels are effective for use in surf fishing. The majority of surf anglers prefer using spinning outfits, as they are easier to use and are less likely to foul. Even the most seasoned veteran will attest that greater casting accuracy is offered by spinning reels. Reel speed rotation is a function of the spool diameter and gear ratio. If you are a novice to the sport of fishing, do not make the mistake of opening and cleaning the inside of your reel. The inside of each and every reel has springs that will pop out of place as soon as you attempt to remove the reel frame. They are nearly impossible to put back into place. Lubrication of your reel's moving components is paramount for proper performance. New fishing reels that come from the factory are shipped with a minimum amount of grease so they are smooth for in-store demonstrations but will not stain the boxes and packaging. Never lay your reel down in the sand, as this is the fastest way to ruin your gear. The same can be said for allowing your reel to become submerged in salt water. Nearly all manufacturers of quality fishing reels discourage submerging your reel under water. Even fresh water can become trapped and lead to equipment failure. Simply rinsing your rod and reels off with a garden hose will suffice. Make a practice to separate your rod and reel at the conclusion of every fishing expedition. When my reels are in need of a deep cleaning to remove mineral buildup, a small amount of kerosene makes for an excellent solvent, but avoid touching any chemicals to your fishing line. Wipe down your reels with a damp cloth and polish dry before storage. I use PENN reels.

SPINNING REELS

Spinning reel.

Spinning or open-face reels are the most popular variety on the market, not only for the experienced anglers but for the novice as well. The majority of people can manage well enough with a spinning reel on their first fishing trip. Moreover, mastering the cast with spinning equipment comes much faster than with conventional reels. This amounts to faster retrieval, minimal foul-up and less downtime on the beach. Always make certain that your bail is in the proper location. Bail trips work with inertia and can be fickle. Some spinning reels are now manufactured without the traditional bail wire. It looks as though these bail-less reels are gaining a foothold with many anglers.

Quality reels will be constructed of stainless steel or graphite components. Make certain when you are spooling your line to your reel that you leave the line about an eighth of an inch below the lip. This will decrease the chances of your line prematurely leaving the spool. Spinning outfits can cast a lighter lure than can a conventional reel. Spinning equipment is not subject to the major headaches associated with line backlash. The correct timing for releasing the line is dependent on where your rig lands. If your rig lands behind you in the sand, you were a bit premature on the release. If your rig lands at your feet then you held on a bit too long. If your rig hits your head then you're getting closer. Release the line from the tip of your index finger when the line pressure is at its peak. Keep your rod pointed in the desired direction of your target area. Spinning reels are fun to use. I use my spinning gear nearly 90 percent of the time when I am surf fishing.

CONVENTIONAL REELS

The conventional or "level wind" reel has been around for over a century. These types of reels are much more difficult for the novice angler to use. Not only do these reels take a lot of practice, but they are still most prone to fouling, better known as "bird nesting." This is the unfortunate event when your line wraps around the spool, creating a mess. Correcting bird nesting requires a lot of patience and time to correct. Nesting usually happens right as the fish starts to run.

Conventional reel.

Always have a spare outfit at hand. Conventional reels are more rugged and less likely to have mechanical failure. Conventional reels are also the tackle of choice for those who fish offshore. They do not work well with the newer type of braided lines. A braided line will "bury" within itself under the force of the cast. Setting the drag to the proper setting is critical. Most conventional reels have a star drag that controls spool rotation with friction. Conventional reels are very versatile and are the standard for freshwater fishing. These reels will intimidate you at first. Spool these reels up with fourteen- to twenty-pound monofilament line. Use your thumb as a brake to control spool rotation speed to feather your rig to ensure a smooth entry into the water. A backlash is an overrun in which the reel spool rotates so fast that the spooled line starts to wind back on itself. This creates small loops that bind the line trying to come off the reel. When this occurs (not *if* this occurs), you will have lost your rig to Davy Jones's locker. In addition, you will get to spend upward of thirty minutes carefully and methodically undoing these nasty loops and knots. Pray that the fish do not start to run while you are in this repair mode. Every conventional reel that I have owned is equipped with a static or click feature to alert you when your spool is in motion.

SETTING THE DRAG

The drag feature on a fishing reel is what keeps your line from breaking under the strain of a fish. The drag works by the angler manually tightening the drag dial, which compresses a series of washers or gaskets. The tighter you set your drag, the more friction is produced. Too often, anglers over-tighten the drag. This can lead to line failure and a lost fish. Allow for the natural resistance of your line being pulled through the water. I was fishing with a group one time when a sizable puppy drum hit my line like a freight train. In this case, my drag was set way too loose. I tried to tighten my drag in the middle of the fight only to have my index finger sliced open to the bone. I attempted to regulate the line directly, while I should have thumbed the spool to make my adjustment. Fishing line pulled with any pressure across your finger will open you right up, particularly braided line.

ALVEY REELS

Australian in origin, these reels are not seen very often in the States. Alvey reels look somewhat like an inverted fly rod reel. They are known for their unbeatable ability in long casting contests. I made a promise to one of my buddies whom I was fishing with in Australia at the Great Barrier Reef that I would mention his native Alvey reel.

Chapter 3

Line, Leaders and Hooks

FISHING LINE

Fishing line comes in a huge variety of colors, materials, size, etc. Using colored line is dictated by where you are fishing, water clarity and location. Many anglers prefer high-visibility lines so that they may follow their cast and sight deployment location once in the surf. Some anglers prefer line that is very limp so that they get a better feel for the action. Cheap fishing line is very inconsistent when it comes to diameter consistency and tensile strength. Also, it becomes brittle very quickly due to susceptibility to ultraviolet degradation of the nylon. Getting in the habit of replacing your fishing line every year is one of the best practices you can adopt. Frayed or brittle line will lead to untimely breaks more often than not. Some anglers use fishing line that is way too strong of test for what they are fishing. Using too heavy of line reduces sensitivity and casting ability, as well as wind interference. Following are the common types of lines used.

Monofilament

This is the original "standard" type of line used in the sport. Monofilament was the primary reason that spinning reels became very popular after World War II. It is the most common of all fishing lines. It has a very low spectrum of visibility in the water. Always check for abrasions and nicks. The best way to check for any problems is to let the line run across your finger when reeling in your line. Be careful not to cut yourself when doing this. If you feel any abrasions or nicks, replace your line. Otherwise, you risk breakage when you have a load (fish) on your line. Monofilament does tend to stretch and become brittle with exposure to the sun's ultraviolet light. Monofilament can become twisted and coiled, which can lead to foul-ups.

Braided Line

I have become a very big fan of braided fishing lines. They are very strong and small in diameter, coupled with extreme test strength—three times the pound strength of equal diameter of monofilament. Braided line is a micro-fiber, polyethylene-based (GSP) material that anglers either love or hate. Braided line affords the angler with a limp, very castable material with minimal wind resistance. It holds knots very well. There is very little stretch or elasticity. Braided line can have a tendency to stick together while being released from the spool. This can lead to fouling of your line during casting. While braided lines are not as susceptible to UV damage, you must inspect for dark spots that appear and could result in line rot. If you change your line each season, you should not have any problems.

Fluorocarbon

This is very expensive line that is used primarily as leader material, being that it does not tend to twist or coil. Fluorocarbon is a very limp line that is excellent for long-smooth casting. Most retailers sell fluorocarbon in large, loose coils in quantities of thirty yards or less. It is highly invisible to fish with the keenest eyesight. Always use a fluorocarbon leader when fishing for species such as speckled trout.

Fishing around structures or debris can be tough on fishing line and leader material. This is especially true if you are fishing with live baits or jig heads. It is highly recommended that you use braid or fluorocarbon, which are more resistant to abrasion. Use fourteen- to seventeen-pound test connected to a leader with a number twelve barrel swivel. Connect this to seven feet of twenty-pound test leader to lessen the chances of line failure.

Using a Leader

Whether it's bluefish, flounder or mackerel, sharp teeth dictate using wire leaders. The downside to using a wire leader instead of a mono leader is that fish can more easily see a wire leader. Some anglers swear by them; others swear at them. Freshwater fishermen rarely use them. The primary reason for using a leader is to prevent your line from breaking during casting or to prevent a fish from chewing through and cutting your line.

Leader Material

Leader material can be almost any type of line that connects your rig or lure to your primary spool line. In addition to the leader providing a tie-on type of connection, the leader is there to prevent fish from chewing or cutting the line with their razor-sharp teeth. I prefer a surgeon's knot to join the leader to the line. Rocks and underwater structures can also cause your line to be severed. Fishing in and around rocks can get very expensive using the wrong type of leader or, worse, using no leader at all. In general, choose a leader that is at least three times your line strength rating. Take the time to tie your own leader. Do not waste your money on store-bought or premade leaders or rigs, as they will probably fail you when you hook any sizable fish. Tying your own rigs is not difficult and is easily mastered after you get the hang of it. Do not waste valuable fishing time tying these on the beach.

Shock Leaders

A shock leader is designed to prevent breakage during the action of casting. As the name implies, shock leader absorbs the brunt of the shock during the cast. Shock leaders also help prevent line breaks from underwater abrasion or being cut from razor-sharp teeth. When casting heavy rigs, fishermen tie a heavier line to the lighter line that is spooled onto the reel. The purpose of doing this is to reduce the possibility of line breakage during the cast. This heavier line is called a shock leader and is usually two to three times greater than the line spooled onto your reel. The attached shock leader material should be long enough to make four to five rotations around the reel's spool. When the rod is loaded during the cast, the heavier shock leader should not fail under the stress of the cast. As soon as the rig is in flight, your regular spooled line will allow for distance and control.

Wire Leaders

These are difficult to tie and can become very easily kinked. Wire leaders do work well with toothy fish such as bluefish. If you want to use a wire leader, consider the limp, tie-able kind such as that manufactured by Tygel. This is the only type of wire leader that I use. You can easily tie it into a knot without using any tools. This limp wire material does not give me any problems with becoming kinked. Given the difficulty of tying leaders and rigs, it is highly recommended that you do so prior to heading out to the beach. The ideal rule of thumb for choosing which pound of test to use is two to three times that of your line. If you are using twelve-pound test line, a leader in the twenty-five- to thirty-pound test range will work well. As a rule, you will catch more fish with a lighter leader than a heavier one.

Spool Backing Material(s)

There is some debate on whether to use some form of backing material when spooling up your line. Backing material is usually a thin layer of sticky back tape or a few wraps of monofilament that wrap around the inside of the reel spool. You need just enough to barely cover the base of the spool. The primary reason to have backing material is to ensure that the body of line clings tightly to the spool. In the event that you deploy all your line during a fight, your line will hold and not spin freely around the spool. Always make certain that the end of your line is securely tied to the spool. I have witnessed on more than one occasion a fish emptying a spool where the line was not secured. Anglers make this mistake only once.

TROUBLESHOOTING GUIDE FOR FISHING LINE

1. Line becomes twisted or coiled
Too heavy of line test for spool size.
Line was left too long in storage.
Not enough line on the spool.

2. Line breaks very easily
Line is nicked, frayed or abraded. Run line carefully between your finger and thumb to feel for damage. Check eyelets and guides for damage.
Line may be brittle from age or exposure to UV light.
Not using heavy enough test.

3. Line is very difficult to see in the water
Consider switching to high-visibility line. Sight your line when casting into the surf.

4. Line is sticky or tacky feeling
Your line was stored in a place where the humidity and temperature are high. Rinse your reel and line before storage.

5. Line is twisted
On the beach, secure your rod in the upright position, take the end of the line and walk seventy-five yards down the beach. Lay the line down, return to your reel and slowly retrieve your line. Hold your line tightly between your thumb and forefinger as you firmly re-spool your line. The best way to prevent line failure is to replace all your line after each season of use.
Always, without exception, invest in a high-quality line, be it monofilament or braid.

Hook Fundamentals

Investing in the highest-quality hooks is a prudent use of your cash. Back in the old days prior to the Industrial Revolution, fishing hooks were nonstandard and often were constructed with a piece of simple wire or other metal byproduct. Prior to the 1800s, people would use animal bone or carved wood to act as a hook. We have come a long way in the sport in regard to how our tackle is made. Saltwater hooks are rated in ascending order of wire diameter: 1) regular, 2) strong, 3) X strong, 4) XX strong.

As the number goes down, the hook size increases all the way down to a number 1 size hook. At this point of measurement, the number changes to the designation of 0s, aka "aught." A hook sized 1/0 is pronounced "one aught." This hook is next larger in size to a hook size 1. In ascending order, the next larger in size is a 2/0. This numbering scheme goes as high as a 19/0 size hook. The complete size designation system looks like this:

Size: smallest from 32, 30, 28, 26, 24, 22, 20, 18, 16, 14, 12, 11, 10, 8, 6, 4, 2, 1, 1/0, 2/0, 3/0, 4/0, 5/0, 6/0, 7/0, 8/0, 9/0, 10/0, 11/0, 12/0, 13/0, 14/0, 15/0, 16/0, 17/0, 18/0, 19/0 being the largest

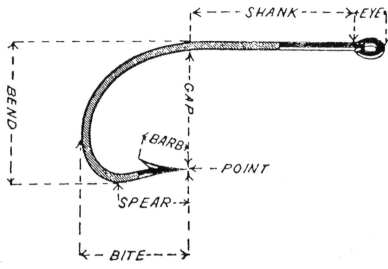

Courtesy of George Poveromo.

Shank Does Matter

The shank portion of the hook is the section of the hook between the eye and the bend. Most types of hooks are available in short, regular or long shank styles. I prefer to use long/extended shank hooks for ease of handling and for faster hook removal from the fish's mouth. Make certain that you use high-quality saltwater hooks. I do not save my used hooks from one trip to another.

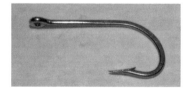

Long-shank hook.

Selecting the proper hook is dependent on several factors. The smaller the fish you are pursuing, the smaller the hook that is required. There is no one-hook-fits-all in surf fishing.

Circle Hooks

These more recently designed hooks are intended to prevent a fish from becoming "gut" hooked. When a fish is hooked within his stomach cavity, the wound is almost always mortal. Researchers confirm that as long as

the hook does not puncture the fish's vital organs, survival is promising. Circle hooks are designed in such a way that they easily slide out the fish's stomach and become lodged in the side of the mouth upon exit. These hooks were first used by long-liner fishermen who were not around to monitor and set the hook. This is accomplished by having the sharp point turned slightly inward toward the gap. The second design change is that the overall hook itself is more rounded, which allows the jaw to become hooked. Circle hooks do work. However, they do not work well if you try to "set" your hook, as has been tradition. I do use circle hooks on all my drum rigs.

Aberdeen Hooks

These hooks are manufactured with thin-gauge wire for primarily smaller-sized game fish. Being of thin diameter, these hooks can bend when forced. Most freshwater hooks are of this construction.

Bronze Hooks

These are the standard for use in freshwater where there is little or no corrosion.

Kahle Hooks

These are similar to circle hooks and are excellent for use with bait such as sand fleas.

O'Shaughnessy Hooks

These are pretty much the big boy's off-surf hooks. They are forged with very strong material that is well suited for saltwater fishing. These hooks will not bend under the pressure of a fish, if using the correct size for the species.

Gamakatsu Hooks

This is an excellent hook series produced in Japan, one of your best buys.

Hook Metallurgy/Geometry

Stainless hooks are a very popular kind of hook. They tend to be very strong and withstand corrosion much better than bronze hooks. Most manufacturers of high-end stainless steel hooks form the product with a nickel/steel alloy for strength and reduced weight.

Never tie a lightweight, thin wire hook onto your rig. I lost a citation doormat flounder on the Avon Pier. After a twenty-minute fight, I pulled in my rig only to find my hook straightened. Big boys do cry. If you plan from the onset to release your catch, you can flatten your barbs to help ensure that your fish can be easily released. The barb of a hook is designed to keep the fish from dislodging the hook during retrieval. Universally, hooks are measured in two dimensions: 1) the gap and 2) length of shank. Saltwater hooks, although varied in composition and design, generally boast a more rugged and corrosion resistance than freshwater versions. Unfortunately, there is no such thing as an "all-in-one" hook. No one hook can meet the requirements for all types of fishing. Proper hook selection is the critical link when fishing with curly tails and other soft plastics. In order to work your lure as to emulate a baitfish, a certain degree of finesse must be employed. Using an oversized hook can cause the lure to separate prematurely and diminish the bait's action. Conversely, a hook that is on the small size can prevent you from setting the hook during the strike. Most surf fishermen deploy soft baits using a jig head.

Every angler should have in his arsenal a variety of hooks and sizes to match his tackle for each type of bait application. There is a hook that works best for each situation and bait. Hook selection is as vital to having well-balanced tackle as is having balanced rods and reels.

Chapter 4

Rigs, Knots and Terminal Tackle

Rigs

I prefer to tie my own rigs and use the absolute minimal amount of hardware. I find it difficult to believe that a laborer tying rigs in an Asian sweatshop is more reliable than me. My rigs are tied moist, and the knots are tipped with superglue to ensure strength.

Good marketing can mean poor fishing. Many of the items that you see in the tackle store are packaged to attract your wallet, not fish. Do not be fooled into thinking that if the tackle shop sells it, it must be good. Au contraire. These shops are in business to make money by moving the most product that gives them the most profit margin.

When purchasing your terminal tackle, make certain that you invest in a quality product. Do not be price sensitive when dealing with your terminal connection tackle. You do not want any of your components to fail you in the field. Consider using a matte finish black if available in what you are shopping for. Deploying a bright, shiny reflective piece of tackle can lead to one of two events, neither of which is favorable: 1) Species such as sea trout are easily spooked by any type of shiny apparatus and will not bite; 2) Other species, particularly bluefish, will often strike at the bright, shiny connector, not the baited hook or lure.

Double-Bottom Rig

Without a doubt, this is the most common type of rig used on the southeastern coast of the United States. More fish are landed with this rig from the surf and the pier. Many times, fish are reeled in two at a time when this rig is deployed. This rig is not only used by beginners but seasoned surfcasters as well. I will often bait one hook with shrimp and the other with bloodworm or squid to ascertain what the fish are hitting. These rigs are simple to make and can be varied as to the type of fish you are pursuing. I prefer to keep excess hardware to a minimum.

Fireball Rig

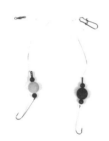

This rig is used most often to catch bluefish. The fluorescent yellow- and red-colored floats serve two purposes: 1) the bright colors tend to attract the blues and 2) the floats help keep your bait suspended from the ocean floor, thus preventing the crabs from harvesting your bait.

Fish-Finder Rig

This rig allows the fish to pick up and sample the bait without being spooked by the resistance of your weight. It requires the use of a sleeved slider weight that allows your rig some unrestricted movement.

Drum Rig

The drum rig is designed to catch large drum. The rig is designed in such a way to accommodate a large enough hook (preferably a circle hook) and leader material strong enough not to break or

lacerate from sharp teeth. Traditionally, the drum rig is assembled with a three-way swivel with one point attached to your line, the second attached directly to your sinker and the third attached to the leader and hook.

Carolina Rig

This is a weight in-line rig that is very popular for fishing pompano, fluke and drum. The rig is assembled with a one-quarter- to one-ounce egg sinker and a Kayle hook affixed to a heavy two- or three-foot leader. Carolina rigs are excellent when fished with live minnows.

Slider Rigs

This rig is similar to the fish-finder rig that allows your weight to move freely along the axis of the rig body. This is important so that the fish will not feel any resistance when they sample your bait. Several species are easily spooked and will quickly abandon the pursuit.

Single-Bottom Rig

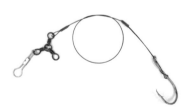

These are single-hook bottom rigs joined with a three-way swivel and a weight. Most single rigs are deployed with a short shank hook or a circle hook.

Flounder Rigs

I deploy several variations of flounder rigs, each dependent on the situation at hand. The spreader rig is excellent for catching flounder in a variety of conditions.

Flounder Pounder and Fluke Killer Rigs

A popular fluke rig using approximately fourteen-pound test line, thin enough to remain somewhat invisible. Fourteen-pound test should handle most any fluke you will hook in the  surf, using a 4/0 hook with eighteen inches of thirty-pound monofilament leader. The best hooks for fishing for flounder have a pretty wide gap that enable the fish to take hold from a bottom position. Deploy this rig with a smooth disc-style weight that will glide smoothly across the sandy bottom. This arrangement works very well when using a three- to four-inch-long, whole finger mullet as bait.

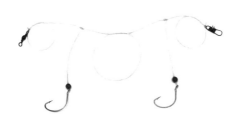

Pompano Rig

This is a specialty rig designed to be used in the surf and baited with sand fleas. Prepare this rig with two bright gold/bronze hooks size #6. These hooks are tied in tandem, with approximately seven inches of header per hook. The weight should be a smooth, coin type of sinker that can ride easily across the sand, much like a flounder rig.

Spec Rig

This rig is ideal for catching speckled trout. Trout have excellent eyesight. Make certain that any hardware is kept to a minimum. This rig is also tied in tandem and uses a minimal amount of weight, as specs can be very finicky in regard to their menu selections. Most spec rigs are constructed with lead jig heads and are tipped with a very small piece of natural or synthetic bait for added scent attraction.

Float Rig

I have had good success in the summer months fishing a float rig with live shrimp. These are best deployed as a large float with a three-quarter-ounce weight, placed ten inches below the float, beaded so as not to interfere with the knots. Attach to a twenty-inch, twenty-five-pound fluorocarbon leader to a number 2 or 4 live bait hook. Hook the live shrimp behind the eyes. These rigs are great for backwater fishing.

Seldom do I use any type of floats while engaged in surf fishing. More often than not, the deployment of a float involves keeping your rig and a free meal off the bottom, away from the crabs. The only other time that I use a float when fishing from the beach is to suspend my offerings slightly below the surface. Most of the time I will deploy a float rig in the backwater sounds or estuaries when fishing live bait such as finger mullet, shrimp or minnows.

Spot-Kingfish Rig

This rig uses smaller hooks with floats for fishing baits such as cut shrimp or bloodworms. These are best when fished with a three-ounce weight. The smaller hooks accommodate the smaller species' mouths.

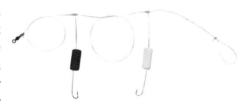

Finger Mullet Rig

This rig is a fairly new product in terms of popularity. This is a prefabricated rig that you will not be able to replicate on your own like most many other rigs. The rig is not that complicated to understand. It affords the angler a

better than average chance of hooking a fish without losing his bait time and again. The rig is connected with a three-way swivel with one connection serving to attach the line, the second for securing your weight and the third attached to the leader with your baited hook. The rig features a heavy mono leader with an inline float. Four inches beyond the float is a heavy gauge wire, which is inserted into the mullet's mouth and exits through the anal opening. The end of the wire has a loop that is used to attach a split-double hook that is attached after the loop exits the anal opening. This rig will allow the angler to cast and redeploy this rig multiple times without having the bait fly off during the cast. Further, the hook is attached in such a way that smaller fish have a difficult time stealing your bait. This is one of the few rigs that I purchase pre-manufactured. Manipulating the heavy-gauge wire and locating the unique split double hooks brought me to this conclusion. Our friends at Sea Striker in Morehead City, North Carolina, distribute my favorite version of this rig.

COMMON FISHING KNOTS

Fishing knots are intended to be pulled extremely tight before use. To ensure that your knot is secure, moisten it with saliva when pulling it tight. This reduces excessive heat generation when the knot is pulled to closure. Many fishing knots are almost identical and are interchangeable. Once your line has developed a knot where the line passes around itself, the line strength is diminished by greater than 50 percent. The tab ends of most fishing can and should be trimmed closely to the knot. Removing the excess tab will reduce the chance of your getting caught up in seaweed and hanging up your rig with your line. The best tool for trimming excess line is a pair of toenail clippers. Many anglers secure their knots with a very small touch of super glue to ensure against slippage. I tend to stick with three or four knots only. I can tie them quickly and properly almost every time. We are not in training for NASA. Master two or three knots and you will be ready to fish. The following are a few of the most popular knots used by surf fishermen. It is a good idea to practice these knots before you need to use them. More often than not, you will become comfortable with certain knots and use them most of the time. All knot images are courtesy of Harry Nilsson.

Palomar Knot

This is the best knot to use with braided lines. It is reliable and easy to tie for terminal tackle connections and lures. I use the Palomar knot exclusively when tying to braided line.

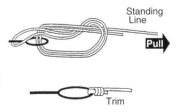

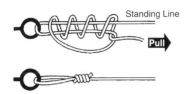

Uni-Knot

This knot is strong and reliable for securing terminal tackle to monofilament.

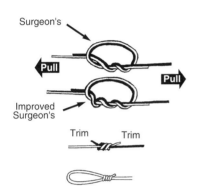

Surgeon's Knot

This is a fast and easy knot for joining leader material to a line with unequal diameters. This knot will rarely fail you when tied properly.

Dropper Loop

This is an excellent knot for forming a loop at any point within the line or leader. It is the most popular loop for making rigs for attaching tackle such as hooks or lead jig heads in tandem.

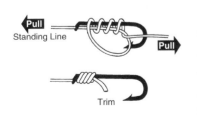

Snell Knot

This is primarily used for snelling line to the shank of a hook. This knot only works well with long shank hooks. It creates a strong, permanent connection between a monofilament leader and a hook.

Blood Knot

This knot is used for joining two sections of line or leader together. It is also used for affixing leader material to line, preferably if both lines are of similar diameter.

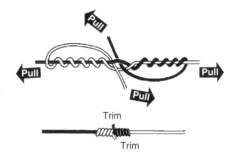

End Loop Knot

This knot is excellent for making a loop at the end of a line. It is ideal for quickly attaching tackle, lures or leaders. This is an excellent knot that works well when operating in conditions that are less than ideal.

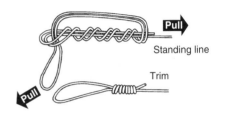

Clinch Knot

This is the most commonly used knot for saltwater fishing. The knot is both reliable and easy to tie very consistently.

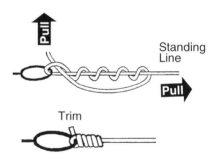

Improved Clinch Knot

This is an excellent, time-tested knot for securing terminal tackle to monofilament. It is reliable and easy to tie and is probably the most common knot used for fishing.

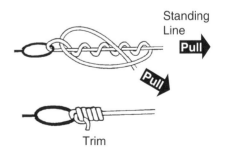

Reel Spool Knot

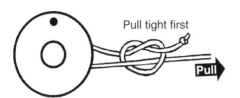

This knot is ideal for properly securing line to your reel spool. A backing material is highly recommended to prevent slippage.

TERMINAL TACKLE

By definition, these are the components that are tied to the end of your fishing line. This includes but is not limited to swivels, hooks, weights, leaders and lures or plugs.

Three-Way Swivels with a Snap Connector

This apparatus is used when a weight is connected directly to the swivel. This tackle is used for drum rigs and single-bottom rigs.

Three-Way Swivels

Three-way swivels have three independently rotating eyes that are attached to a center ring. These are among the most basic pieces of tackle that every surf fisherman should carry in his tackle box.

Swivels

The primary function of any type of swivel is to allow the terminal tackle the freedom to spin while keeping your line from twisting. The movement of water on your rig or the rotation

of your lures can twist your line and foul your tackle. There are several different types of swivels on the market. The barrel swivel is the standard.

A single-swivel has two independently rotating eyes that are attached to a center ring. The newer generation of swivel is the ball-bearing swivel. The ball-bearing swivel is more of a high-performance piece that rotates very smoothly without sticking. Gravitate toward using ball-bearing swivels when fishing with artificial lures.

Snap Connectors

Snaps come in a multitude of varieties. Their primary function is to allow for fast connect or disconnect of lures and rigs. Most models of snaps have a thing or two in common, including that they are most difficult to open and close with wet fingers. The following are the most popular varieties of snap connection devices.

Duo-Lock

This is my favorite snap device because it is a dependable, secure and easy-to-use connection apparatus.

Coast-Lock

This is similar to the duo-lock system with a slightly different closure.

Cross-Lock

The cross-lock is well designed to open and close with ease. This style of snap works well when conditions are wet and cold.

Figure-Eight Sinker Connectors

The old-style figure-eight connectors are an absolute bitch to use. Usually, you will have to resort to using your pliers to force them open and close. They are commonly used with cheap, store-bought rigs. I often switch out these connectors with a duo-lock and dispose of the faulty parts. Do not waste your time or your money using figure-eight connectors.

Twist-n-Lock Slide Connectors

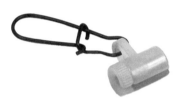

This is a new type of sinker slide that allows you to add a sliding weight to any rig without cutting and retying your line. These are equipped with a duo-lock snap. They are a highly recommended addition for every tackle box.

Snap Swivels

Snap swivels are just that. They combine both the snap and the swivel. These are also a staple that every angler should have in his tackle box.

Sleeves

Sleeves are small, hollow barrels that are used to join two material lines together. Sleeves are almost always used when working with steel leader material. Your line is fed into the sleeve together and crimped with a tool that will bind the lines together, thus preventing separation. Use caution not to overkill your crimp, as you can cut or weaken your line if you crimp too closely to the edge or apply too much force when squeezing.

WEIGHTS AND SINKERS

Lead sinkers or weights have been used in the sport forever. They get the job done. Because of undercurrents and wave action, it is usually necessary to use a lead weight to ensure that your rig holds in place on the bottom. The only negative that has arisen from their use is a warning in regard to lead interaction with the environment. Yes, lead is heavy and must be transported to and from the beach. However, using a lead weight is the only way to keep your bait stable in the surf. In addition, your weight affords you the ability to cast your load. It requires some effort to pull your line off the spool and send it one hundred yards into the ocean. Most surf fishermen will use between three and five ounces of lead coupled with fifteen- to thirty-pound test line.

Pyramid Sinker

This is the most popular and common type of weight used for surf fishing based on sales and experience from up and down the coast. The three-ounce weight is used most often.

Bank Sinkers

Bank sinkers are used when underwater obstructions are present. Several fishing piers along the Grand Strand have rock- and coral-type formations that will snag and retain any rig not equipped with the "rounded" bank-style sinker.

Disc Weights

Also known as disc sinkers, these are used for the most part when bait presentation requires mobility, i.e., slow retrieve, as when fishing for flounder or spec (trout). The flatness of the weight affords the angler the ability to avoid a rough retrieve and/or line twist when working the rig through the surf.

Egg Sinkers

Egg-type sinkers are in-line weights, meaning that they are not affixed and can move up and down with the current to some degree. The most common type of rig using this setup is the Carolina rig. This rig allows the fish to pick up the bait for a taste while not filling the resistance of a weight. Several species of fish can detect resistance and can become spooked.

Storm Sinkers

This new type of sinker originates from Great Britain, where the surf is always tumultuous. Storm sinkers are nicknamed "spud nick weights" because they have four wire appendages that hold the weight firmly into place in rough seas. The four wires are spring-loaded and will disengage with a snapping action that will release the hold of the wire anchors. I am not a fan of these weights. If the surf conditions are too rough for my six- or eight-ounce weights, then it is time to back it in.

Tongue Weights

These sinkers are one of the newest types being used in the surf. They somewhat resemble a frog's mouth. They tend to hold quite well in the surf, as they dig in to the bottom better than does the pyramid style.

In-Line Weights

In-line weights are elongated, with each end having a terminal ring connection. This feature allows you to add weight on the line directly.

Choosing the correct weight is of the utmost importance. The two primary goals of the weight or sinker are as follows:

1. To place your rig in the desired target location in the surf.

2. To hold your rig in place at the desired location. Using too little weight will allow your rig to drift with the current. Usually, this means that your rig will end up down the beach in a foot or two of water. Using too heavy weight will hinder your ability to feel the action or strike. This usually results in lost bait and no fish. When fishing on a beach with little or no slope, the fish will tend to congregate in four to six feet of water, providing that there is enough water turbulence to stir up the baitfish. Use a heavier weight sinker in this circumstance.

Chapter 5

Bait and Lures for Saltwater Fishing

NATURAL FISHING BAIT

Fish feed by sight and smell, so always keep fresh bait on your rig and replace washed-out bait as it loses its scent. Fishing with live bait is better than fresh bait and beats any frozen bait. Using fresh, active bait will consistently produce more fish. I continue to have very regular success fishing with worms. Generally, bloodworms work the best. You must be careful with their heads, which are equipped with pinchers that love fingers. Yes, they draw blood. Warm water depletes the oxygen level in your bait bucket and will result in lifeless minnows. Keep all baits out of the sun in the shade and away from the seagulls.

As a rule, natural bait is more common and generally more productive than artificial bait in the surf. The key is understanding what your targeted species finds naturally appealing. Choosing the correct bait is very much dependent on knowing what is available in the water at any given time.

Shrimp

When using shrimp as bait, I prefer fresh, not frozen. I toughen up my shrimp by submerging them in a cold salt brine solution. The salt draws out the moisture, which toughens the shrimp, allowing your bait to stay in place on the hook. Whether you leave the shell on or remove it is your own choice.

I have heard both sides of the discussion. Yes, it is true that shrimp that fish consume in the wild will have their shells intact. Others argue that by removing the shell, fish can more easily taste the meat and smell the allure. I generally peel my shrimp prior to baiting them on the hook. Baiting your shrimp, shell on, requires a bit more patience in getting the hook through the shell. I find that the shell will come off on its own with little or no effort. As far as fresh shrimp go, the tail portion holds the strongest, most concentrated scent. I have caught more fish using cut shrimp than any other type of bait.

When fishing live shrimp, run the hook ever so carefully between the shrimp's eyes and brain. The brain is located behind the eyes and is identified by two dark spots. Fishing with live shrimp suspended above the bottom has salvaged several outings.

Bloodworms

You can purchase your night crawlers on your way down to the beach, saving money on those expensive bloodworms sold at the bait shop. We try to purchase night crawlers from the inland freshwater bait shops. They are bigger and often more tempting than salt marsh or bloodworms. Always keep your worms stored out of the sun in your cooler to maintain freshness. Bloodworms are very temperamental and must be kept out of the sun in damp seaweed. Exposure to fresh water from melted ice in your cooler will kill your worms. Bloodworms are harvested from the salt marshes and are acclimated to the salinity of the ocean water. Once you have used a bloodworm, do not place it back in with the others, as this will shorten the life of the virgin bait. Bloodworms should be kept in the refrigerator overnight or for an extended time. You will learn over time which baits work best for you. I do fish with a lot of bloodworms and find them to be very productive.

Minnows

These are excellent for flounder in and around structures such as piers, bridges and docks. Mud minnows work well when hooked through the lips. Minnows need to be kept in a saltwater container, preferably with an aerator. If you do not have an aerator, refresh with seawater every few hours. Redfish love feeding on minnows, mullet, menhaden, shrimp, crabs or herring.

Flounder prefer pursuing a beaded, buck-tailed flounder rig tipped with a small offering of fresh-cut bait. Save walking to and from the bait cooler every time you lose your bait. When fishing with shrimp or worms, keep enough to re-bait three or four times in a sealable baggie in your pocket. When re-baiting in the water, be careful not to let your reel become submerged by a rogue wave. Tuck the fore-grip of your rod tightly under your arm so that your reel is secure against the back of your shoulder. Allow for enough slack to bring your rig forward to reload. This simple trick will help you conserve energy for a full day of fishing.

Work your offering bait. Feeding fish can more easily sight a potential meal working against the current. Try to work your lures or bait in a direction opposing the wave action or flow of the current. Species of fish that feed along a beach with little or no slope will tend to congregate in the three- to five-foot depth range as long as there is some water turbulence present.

Cut Bait

Most any type of creature harvested from the sea can suffice as bait. Fish are the most commonly used cut bait. Smaller mullet and spot are among the most common species that are sacrificed for bait. Strips of white flounder belly are excellent bait as well. Anglers who deploy a chunk of cut bait usually do so with a larger hook in hopes of catching a sizable drum, striper or bluefish. Fishing this type of big load can land anything and everything. Sharks are frequently reeled in when deploying a large cut bait rig. Make certain that you afford the weight of your cut bait with your sinker when casting your load so as not to break your rod. Frozen mullet is probably the hardest bait to work with. Avoid using it if at all possible. The flesh easily detaches from the skin, which renders it practically useless.

Sand Fleas

Also known as mole crabs, they tend to congregate in colonies. Ever notice that right as a wave washes out, you see little, inverted V formations in the sand? These are created by sand fleas that are burying themselves back into the sand. These are excellent bait for flounder and pompano. They can be scooped out of the sand with a sand rake or even an old kitchen colander.

They will keep in a bucket of damp sand for hours. Generally, they will remain on the hook for two to three casts at the most. Freshly caught sand fleas stay on hooks pretty well. Many diehard pompano enthusiasts will collect a sizeable harvest of sand fleas when they are most bountiful in late summer and freeze away a supply for winter fishing, as they are not readily available in the winter months. You can flash this frozen bait in boiling water for ten seconds (the color turns to a pinkish orange) and then run them under cold water quickly. This will toughen your bait and help it stay on your hook during casting.

Finger Mullet

Three- to four-inch whole finger mullet are well suited for catching puppy drum, big flounder and large bluefish. The special finger mullet rig is the best rig in my box. About half the time, finger mullet can be caught with a cast net in the surf or in the tidal creeks.

Lures

Below are the essential artificial lures that every surfcaster should have in his arsenal:

- Stingsilvers
- Hopkins: shorties with buck tails
- buck tail jigs: chartreuse and white
- MirrOlure: red and white, green and yellow
- Kast Master Spoons: gold and silver
- Gotcha Plugs: white with a red head
- Roster Tail Spinner
- curly tails: pink and white, green
- Diamond Jigs (gold): excellent for Spaniards and blues
- Clarkspoons
- lead jig heads
- synthetic bait (Berkley Gulp)

Certain species of saltwater game fish are very enticed at the sight of an artificial lure. The species favoring this bait the best are speckled trout, blues, red drum, stripers and Spanish mackerel. Small red drum are frequently mixed in with speckled trout. These two prime species will often be caught at the same time with the exact same baits. Deploying lead head in the one-quarter- to three-quarter-ounce range is very productive for these species. I exclusively fish for specs with artificial lures, primarily a lead head with a curly tail grub retrieved with an erratic jerking fashion. The color pattern that is most productive is the red/white combination. Fishing lures are available in all shapes and sizes. Most are armed with treble hooks, while some have a single hook. The hook arrangement is an important factor in regard to how you are working your lure. Lures with single hooks tend to hold on to the fish better than treble hooks. The downside is that the hook must be pretty much inside the fish's mouth for a solid hook-up. Treble hooks will afford you a better chance of setting the hook on the initial strike. Treble hooks do have the tendency to pull free easier from the fish's mouth.

Single-Hook Lures

These single-hook versions afford two major advantages over using treble hooks. First, single-hooked spinners can be easily fitted with a grub tail or similar soft plastic twister. Second, it is much easier to remove a single shanked hook from a fish than a treble hook. I fit about half of my hooks with a red or yellow buck tail dressing as a teaser.

PRESENTATION OF LURES

Fishing with artificial lures is very favorable during low tide when the surf is out. Baitfish tend to be more concentrated in deeper water during low tide. When the tide begins to change back to an incoming flood tide, they scatter and feed on natural baits over the shoals and flats. Angling for fish using artificial lures requires more skill and patience than fishing with live natural or cut bait. Successfully presenting a lure to the fish is considerably more challenging. Fishing with a lure seems to lull you into a pattern of autopilot. Each lure is designed to mimic a species of baitfish. Some require a fast retrieval, while others may call for a slower rising and falling display.

There is a methodology that goes with using lures and artificial baits. One of the big advantages to using artificial lures is that you can cover a lot of water in a short amount of time. This is achieved by casting your lure using a fan-like motion to maximize coverage. When casting your lure with this motion, work from right to left to more naturally imitate how baitfish swim with the tide. Game fish are not unlike humans in that they prefer the path of least resistance. They will seek out the baitfish that appear to be weak or wounded. Predator fish can spot the injured bait because they tend to distinguish themselves from the rest of the school. Wounded fish do not swim straight and fast but tend to stop and go or swim with a lack of intensity. The fish that moves with an erratic movement poses more of a challenge to the game fish timing a strike. Fishing your lure in a manner so as to imitate a wounded fish will provide more strikes.

Improper retrieval patterns are the biggest culprit for missed strikes when fishing with lures. Many fishermen prefer to work an artificial straight back with little or no variance in action or speed. This will afford you the ability to cover more water in attempting to locate the fish. However, lures and bait that knife straight through the water appear to be fast and healthy. When a fish does strike a lure worked in this fashion, chances are that you will have a solid setting of the hook.

The majority of strikes will come when your lure is on the down stroke. When you are fishing with a floater type of lure, retrieve your lure in a cadence. You want to imagine that your lure is acting like an injured fish in the water. In other words, turn your crank six or seven rotations and let your lure rest. The floaters will ascend to the surface while the sinkers will descend toward the bottom. This movement best resembles a wounded fish. It's when you will get the vast majority of your strikes when using artificial bait.

Floater/Diver Lure

This lure is designed to float to the surface at rest and dive below the surface when retrieved. Swimming plugs are very effective when worked over rocky bottoms. This is accomplished with the plastic bill located in the front of the lure where the lower lip would be. These are very effective lures, as the action of floating and diving looks like a baitfish in distress. Our target game fish will go for this easier, lower-hanging fruit given the chance.

Surface Plugs

These are engineered to float on the surface. Again, this is a visible offering to the game fish. This family of lure is usually elongated for aerodynamics and easy of cast. This is important in that these lures are lighter in weight and can be difficult to cast. There are several ways in which to retrieve these lures for different results. Try a slower, more erratic retrieval.

Popping Plugs

Poppers are lures that float on the surface. They feature a concave face that creates a disturbance on the surface that attracts fish. These are an excellent option when the water is slack or calm. I do not retrieve these very fast but rather slowly, with my rod tip held up.

Metal Spoons

These were probably the first artificial lures developed. They are quite simple and rugged in design. This concave or elongated slab of metal featuring a distinctive wobbling motion produces a bright, reflective light. They are retrieved through the water with a variety of methods. Most are festooned with a treble hook with or without dressing. Another definite advantage of using a spoon is the propensity to cover the water. In the past, fishing with a bladed bait referred to using a metal spoon. These baits have evolved in recent years to encompass a multitude of lures. New hybrids that combine color with versatility are the tackle box standard. The most popular type of spoon is fitted with a split ring to a treble hook. The other style deploys a welded hook that works well not to snag as much saltwater vegetation.

Sinker Lures

These are heavy, deep-running lures that descend as soon as they hit the water. Sinkers can be cast a country mile with very little effort. They, too, are armed with a treble hook. Sinkers can be used in a multitude of ways depending on how fast you retrieve it through the water. The rate of retrieval determines the depth that these lures obtain. These lures are most prone to getting hung up on underwater debris.

Spinners

These lures are designed to attract game fish with vibration and a resonating flash. The blade rotates when properly retrieved through the water. This family of lure usually has a treble hook with or without dressing. I am particularly fond of using a three-quarter-ounce rooster tail in the surf. Spinner baits first gained solid interest among freshwater enthusiasts pursuing largemouth and striped bass. Many types of spinning lures rotate when retrieved, causing your line to twist and tangle.

Lead Jig Heads

These lures feature a weighted lead head with a fixed hook. Jigs are always dressed with feathers, curly tail grubs or buck tail hair. I prefer to "tip" each hook with a small piece of synthetic bait such as Berkley Gulp. A piece the size of your  fingernail will suffice. Any larger of a piece can disrupt the intended action of the lure. These lures come in a variety of sizes and colors. Jigs are one of the most productive lures in my arsenal. They can be used in a variety of ways. Increasing or decreasing your cranking speed when you retrieve will determine whether your bait is near the top or the bottom. Reeling faster will cause the lure to swim close to the surface. Conversely, slowing down your rate of retrieval will cause your bait to swim closer to the bottom. I prefer the rounded lead heads in chartreuse, state red or yellow. When I affix a curly tail plastic grub, I invert the tail opposite the normal direction of upright. This tends to afford an action that is well received. Quite often, I tie two of these in tandem when fishing for speckled trout. One popular method of presenting this bait is to sweep your rod parallel to the surface of the water. This action will let your lure skip across the water prior to sinking below the surface. Another effective method of using these baits is to allow the lure to drag the bottom ever so slightly, stirring up a little bit of sand as it slides across the bottom. Jig heads are one of the most versatile lures in your tackle box.

Swimbaits/Curly Tails

These are another variation used with the lead jig head. Swimbaits are keel weighted so that the lead weight is formed into the bottom of the lure's belly. This distribution of weight keeps the hook in the upright position. This design is engineered so that the bait has built-in swimming action.

Chapter 6

Proper Attire and Essential Accessories

Packing the right clothes for your trip is paramount. Each year for nearly the past decade, I have taken about twenty of my closest friends fishing to Wrightsville Beach. As you can imagine, planning a trip of this magnitude requires months of preparation. Our dates are set in stone six months in advance. We do not have the luxury of canceling or postponing a scheduled trip due to the weather. We fish in the rain, cold and heat. Being a family man requires getting a hall pass from the wife and time off from the office. The only circumstance that would force us to consider bailing would be in the event of a major hurricane, and it would have to be directly on top of our scheduled venue. If you show up at the coast a day or two after a big storm, you will be dealing with beach erosion and heavy amounts of seaweed. Trying to fish with an abundance of seaweed in the water will drive you mad. The problem is that we have no way of knowing what the weather will hold until a day or so before our departure. We always go during the last weekend of October or the first weekend in November. Sometimes, the weather is still quite warm; other times, it is rather cold. Usually, the mornings are chilly and the afternoons are warm. Sunset brings the return of cooler temperatures.

How to pack? Well, we pack plenty of clothes to adjust to the ever-changing conditions. As it turns out this time of year, the water temperature stays warmer than the cool air and will keep your bare feet rather comfortable.

PROPER OUTER WEAR

Stay Light and Stay Dry

Maybe it is just me, but I really do not like the feeling of being bound by bulky clothes. I always dress in layers, ready to peel off the extras as temps warm up. I do carry a light water-resistant rain jacket with a hood for those summer squalls. Pay attention to the color of clothes you choose to wear. We do not want to advertise our approach to the shore. Avoid bright-colored clothing, as there is still debate on whether fish can become spooked by loud colors.

Shorts

Given the opportunity, I wear shorts as often as possible. The only time this really is not possible is January through March. I have a high tolerance to cold. I do suggest that you wear shorts that have a belt loop for your pliers and knife and that your shorts be made of a fabric that will dry quickly. Cabela's and Bass Pro Shops have these shorts.

Sandals

I have been very fortunate in that in my many years of fishing I have not split my foot open like so many of my friends. Stepping on a shell or, worse, a stinger will ruin your trip. I always wear sandals, Keens or Crocs when I am on the beach.

Gloves

The only time I have ever considered using gloves is when I go out deep-sea fishing. Veteran surf fishermen will snicker when the gloves come out. Don't be a sissy.

Hat and Neck Wear

While I really do not enjoy wearing any type of hat, I find that you can really benefit from the protection it offers from the sun, in addition to using sunscreen. The hat that I do wear is butt ugly and has a neck flap that keeps my neck from burning. My appearance when fishing in the dog days of summer resembles that of a German officer in Erwin Rommel's Afrika Corps with the desert flap hat, baggy khaki shirt and shorts. While I may not be netting fish in this intense heat, at least I look damn spiffy!

Waders

I hate them. Try walking for thirty minutes in a set of waders through the soft sand and you'll quickly understand the meaning of misery. Let us not forget, you will be weighted down with carrying all your gear. If you must wear them, slather up with talc powder to prevent chafing, and pack bandages and ointment to treat the rubbing and chafing that accompany wearing waders. They are needed when the water temperature is too cold for you to tolerate. Do not plan on trying to stay dry when the water is cold. The rogue wave will find you for certain and leave you damp and cold. That being said, here are your choices:

HIP WADERS: When I am forced to wear any type of waders, these are what I settle with. Hip waders are separate, boot-type legions that cover each leg up to your crotch. Wearing the waders by themselves without heavy boots can reduce the agony and discomfort associated with these torture devices. I am fortunate that I am able to stand at the water's edge, in water no more than two feet, and cast beyond the breakers.

WAIST WADERS: These are one piece that comes up to just below your beltline. Truth be told, my belly is not very petite. I do not like to wear anything that is tight or that may make me feel more robust than I already am. I am six feet, four inches tall. Hip and waist waders will afford you decent yet cumbersome mobility on the beach.

CHEST WADERS: The first time that I was looking into waders, chest waders were all that I could locate. My knowledge regarding waders was limited. I learned on my first trip why chest waders are also known as "widow makers." It works like this. Being all cozy and warm, we tend to wade out as far as we can so that we may cast farther out and be at one with the fish. One wave is all that it takes to come over the top of your chest waders. They fill with water in about three seconds. There you are in five feet of water with your gear. You will have a very difficult time standing, much less walking and trying to get back. I was a lifeguard in college and struggled with assistance to get back to the beach. That was the last time I will ever don a pair of chest waders with no belt. If you elect to wear chest waders, you must use a chest safety belt to keep water from filling up these pants. Wading of any type can be dangerous. Always wear a flotation belt or similar device when wearing chest waders.

NEOPRENE V. DRY-LOCK: These are the two most popular materials used in the manufacture of waders. The Neoprene is the rubber type, while the Dry-Lock is the lightweight, easy-to-put-on style. Make certain that you rinse thoroughly with fresh water. Allow to thoroughly air dry, hanging inside out with soles up. Never store in the trunk of your car or attic, where excessive heat will ruin your waders.

TOOLS AND HARDWARE

If you must choose which two tools to purchase first, get your high-quality pliers and knife. I made the decision several years ago to use only stainless steel tools for my fishing needs. It really pays to go with higher-end tools. You do not want to be on the beach during a blitz only to discover that your pliers are corroded or the cutter is not clean and won't work. I searched high and low to find a pair of quality pliers that would consistently cut thin-diameter monofilament without hesitation. To determine if the pliers

that you are considering purchasing will work, hold the cutting joint up to the light. If any light is getting through at the cutting joint, chances are they will not cut your line cleanly. My pliers are manufactured by Calcutta and my knife by Henckel.

In addition, be sure to bring along the following tools and hardware:

- Needle-nose pliers: An elemental and absolute must. Keep them at your side always.
- Bait knife: Another absolute must. Very sharp and ready at hand.
- Fish scaler: Optional; you can use almost anything. (I once used a credit card.)
- Hand towels: Keep one on your belt and one at your bait station. An old washcloth works very well.
- Fillet knife: Fillet knives are supposed to be very sharp. They are intended to be used to cut and dress your fish in preparation for table fare. Never use your fillet knife for cutting your bait, as this will quickly dull your edge and render your knife useless for filleting purposes. Invest in high quality cutlery.
- Toenail clippers: Keep a pair for cutting monofilament. These are larger than fingernail clippers and are easier to locate and use. Use a small piece of sandpaper to rough up the top and bottom in order to prevent slippage. Secure with a bright-colored lanyard for easy access.
- Crimping tool: You can use your needle-nose pliers if you have to.
- Steel leader cutter: If you invested in a real nice pair of needle-nose pliers, they will work.
- Small LED light: Nighttime will sneak up on you even if you do not plan to fish in the dark. You can scan the area to ensure that you have collected all your belongings. A very popular item on the market is the lights that attach to your hat. These are readily available and provide sufficient light to operate in the dark.
- Lanyards: Anything and everything that I can affix a lanyard (cord) to, I do. Use bright neon color so that you can locate them if they fall in the sand.
- Maintenance: Once again, always clean each tool you use with warm, soapy water. Make certain that you dry and polish each accessory before storing.

Most everyone carries a cellphone or Blackberry type of device. Seal it up air tight in a Ziploc baggie. This will keep out sand and water. There are certain other items that are must-haves for surf fishing:

BEACH CHAIR: Purchase a chair that is stable and comfortable yet easy to transport. At the end of each trip, spray the hinged joints with WD-40.

SUNSCREEN: Best applied prior to getting on the sandy beach; for lip balm, use a leash that attaches to your front pocket.

HAT: A must. Be certain it is affixed with a lanyard to your shirt collar to prevent loss.

SUNGLASSES: Another must; the glare from the beach and sand will greatly reduce visibility.

FOUL-WEATHER GEAR: Judgment call here. You will only need it if you don't have it.

WADERS: Only needed when the water temperature is too cold for you to tolerate. Do not plan on trying to stay dry when the water is cold. The rogue wave will find you for certain and leave you damp and cold.

FOOTWEAR: Highly recommended that you have some type of footwear on for protection. Heavy-duty sandals such as Keens or Crocs are excellent choices. Stepping on a sharp, broken shell will lacerate your tread enough to end your trip.

TRASH BAG: Always keep your trash secure so that the wind will not carry it away. This applies to everything—discarded fishing line, food wrappers, drink bottles, cigarette butts, etc. You must make certain that you never lose any terminal tackle with a hook attached. It would be most unfortunate for someone's child to step on a hook inadvertently left in the sand. Always carry everything from the beach that you brought with you. Be a good citizen and pick up any other trash that you see. We owe it to ourselves, the environment and future generations to be active custodians of our environment. Ensure that your trash bag stays in place. Put a scoop or two of sand in your trash bag to prevent it from blowing away.

TACKLE BOXES AND BAGS: Many choices are available when it comes to a tackle box. The term "tackle box" is a bit of a misnomer in that the popular tackle boxes of the day are usually soft-sided bags with various compartments for storage. The modern tackle bag affords you quick access with large, zippered pockets. Make certain that your tackle bag has a comfortable shoulder strap. You will see a variety of bags and sizes at the tackle store. Some are large enough to store a Mini Cooper, while others are no more than a small belt attachment. Choose the bag that is right for you. Consider the weight and distances you will have to transport your gear down the beach. I prefer a medium bag about the size of a car battery to take to the beach. I have several larger bags at home for storage and supplies. Proper planning will keep you well prepared for what to transport to the beach. Before each fishing expedition, go through your tackle bag to clean and organize your gear. Discard any rusted, tangled or worn-out supplies. Remember, be organized and ready to fish as soon as you hit the beach. Having your rigs pre-tied and weights accessible will let you get your lines wet without delay.

EYEWEAR ESSENTIALS: Sunglasses are as essential for fishing as are your rod and reel. Eyewear reduces glare and helps clarify the contrast of objects in and on the water. Quality polarized glasses offer the most protection and are the only way to go. Lens color greatly influences how UV light bands pass through to the eye. No matter which style of sunglasses you wear, be certain that they are properly secured with a lanyard. Make certain that you protect your eyewear from sand and any possible impact damage. The descriptions below are general characteristics of available sunglasses:

Gray lens: Probably the most popular colored sunglasses in use. They minimize color distortion and enhance contrast. They are good, general-purpose glasses in minimum-glare environment.

Amber lens: Perform very well on overcast or cloudy, rainy days. They improve visual contrast in almost every outdoor situation.

Sunrise lens: These are more high-performance lenses that provide optimum contrast in low-angle light, such as early sunrise and sunset.

Vermillion lens: High-performance lenses that heighten visual acuity and color enhancement. These lenses afford the brightest and clearest field of vision. Excellent for sight fishing.

Blue-green mirror lens: These shades are better suited for driving than fishing. These types of lenses are designed with the mirror being encased inside the lenses. Blue mirror lenses do perform well when fishing offshore in the brightest of sun.

Sand Spikes: The Long and Short of It

You need to have a sand spike for each rod that you bring to the beach. A sand spike is a piece of cut PVC or any device that keeps your rod upright and out of the sand. You will need your sand spike to hold your rod in place while you are baiting up or changing lures. Most anglers use a sand spike to hold their rod in position while their rig is out in the water waiting for a strike. This works fine as long as you keep a very close watch for any rod movement. With time, you will be able to detect a nibble from the natural action of the current and waves on your rod. If you see everyone's rod slowly moving in precise unison, that would be the natural action of the waves and current. The sand spike of choice is approximately four feet long, made of PVC pipe and has a cut, tapered edge that goes into the sand. Do not bother with the short spikes that will allow your rod and reels to fall over into the sand. At all costs, keep your reels out of the sand. Being tall, I prefer the longer, four-foot version of sand spikes for ease of access and to ensure a deep burial in the sand. Do not waste your money on store-bought sand spikes that are fewer than two feet long. You will have the unpleasant experience of seeing your reel hit the sand come the first substantial strike or, worse, wash out from incoming water. Make your own out of PVC for a third of the price. Purchase an eight-foot section of PVC and cut once in the middle at a forty-five-degree angle. Lightly sand both ends to remove the burrs. Write your name on them, and off you go. Twist, don't hammer, into the sand. You do not want to haul a heavy object to the beach to use a hammer. The experienced angler will use the "press, twist and turn" technique to properly set his sand spikes. You will want your spikes set at a seventy-five-degree angle toward the surf. Make sure that they are set with at least one-third of the length in moist sand. Rinse off your sand spikes after each trip to the water's edge. This will help reduce the amount of sand you collect in your vehicle. Always be sure that your sand spike is firmly secure. Keep a close eye on the incoming tide so as not to allow the water to reach your spike. Your rod will be under stress when baited and deployed. One pass of water from the incoming tide will topple over any poorly secured outfit.

Keep your tackle high and dry. Back way off on the drag, as a sharp hit and strong run can bring your rod into the water. I have been on two expeditions during which entire rods and reels have been pulled over and out to sea due to washout from having too short of spikes, not to mention the fisherman failing to tend to his gear. On both occasions, the angler blamed his misfortune on a large fish. If you are ever in this sad and embarrassing situation, embellish your plight as well.

NETS AND GAFFS

The purpose of using a net is twofold: 1) The majority of fish are lost during the transition time of bringing your fish out of the water into the cooler; and 2) Using a net will usually afford the fish less stress if you plan to release. Not having to pick up by hand and risk the encounter with sharp teeth is an added bonus.

Cast Nets/Seines

The cast net is very useful in providing you with fresh, natural bait. Many times, the bait shop will not have the desired fresh native bait you seek. I use a monofilament cast net as opposed to the corded variety. The monofilament nets are less visible in the water and tend to open faster than braided nets.

Landing Nets

Landing nets are much friendlier to fish than gaffs. Rinse out your nets with fresh water and allow to dry completely in the sun. Allow your nets to dry out prior to folding and storing. If the nets are not free of all debris and moisture, they will mold and mildew.

Phiester

A small club that resembles a very short baseball bat used to subdue a dangerous fish or to discourage others from lifting your chilled libations. Phiesters are used most commonly on offshore sport-fishing boats.

Surf Gaff

For fishing in the surf, one only needs a small eighteen- to twenty-inch gaff. It is much preferred that you use a landing net instead of a gaff. Unless you are determined to keep your fish for consumption, do not deploy a gaff. The gaff will always result in a mortally wounded fish. You will learn with experience to let the wave wash your fish up onto the beach for you.

CASHING IN ON CAST NETS

Learn to toss a cast net properly and you will save a fortune at the bait store. With a bit of practice, you can become quite proficient with using a cast net. Throwing a cast net can be mastered after several trips to the water. Simply fasten the rope to your right wrist while gathering the extra rope into medium coils in your right hand. Grab the net tightly, about one-quarter of the way down. Allow the remainder of your net to back over your right hand. Extend your right arm and take hold of the forward-most lead weight with your left hand. Reach down to the bottom of the net and grasp closely, pulling just enough to form a horizontal line across your chest. Position both of your feet in line with your intended direction of net placement. Rotate your body clockwise about half a turn momentarily. Lead with your left hand while moving counterclockwise during the toss. Allow your right hand to follow your left while lowering your swing with your left hand and pull slightly while raising your extended right hand for release. With this action, you are actually throwing the net with your right arm. The net will then start to pull slightly and begin to open. Using your wrist, give it a final quick spin while fully releasing your right hand, followed by your left. At this point, your net should be fully deployed while descending toward the water. Your net will remain open as it sinks. Wait about five seconds before gathering the rope back in. I have witnessed many a seasoned angler toss a cast net and gather a day's worth of fresh, live bait. Here are a few of the basics when using a cast net: 1) When starting out, choose a small six-footer size for minnows and small mullet; 2) After use or exposure to salt water, pick out all remaining gilled baits and debris. Rinse your net thoroughly with fresh water; 3) Allow your net to dry completely by spreading it out in the shade and letting it air dry; 4) Store your net in a sealable plastic bucket to keep out the sun's ultraviolet rays. Overexposure to the harsh ultraviolet light will lead to premature breakdown of the net's fabric material. Lastly, at least once a season, fill the plastic storage bucket with fresh water and a quarter cup of fabric softener. Let the net soak overnight and then dry as usual. Caring for your net will afford you many seasons of service. Please remain cognizant not to keep any more baitfish than you intend to use. It is the responsibility of every angler to be a good steward of our environment and our precious natural resources.

BEACH CARTS AND TACKLE BUGGIES

Each year, more and more beachfront is closed off to motor vehicles. I do not foresee a reversal in this trend. More efforts are being made on the state and national levels to protect endangered species of birds and sea turtles. This leaves us with very little choice if we want to fish. Don't dread having to lug your heavy beach cart down the beach. While it is so easy to pull any cart over a hard surface, it will become apparent within the first fifteen feet of soft sand how difficult this truly is. Some refer to this as the oceanic death hike. You would become utterly worn out before you reached your set-up spot. Do not think about trying to lug all your gear through the soft sand while wearing waders. Here are some other pointers and essentials:

- Go lightweight: Carry as little as possible to the water's edge.
- Balloon tires: An absolute must to displace the sand and keep your cart from sinking.
- Tie downs: For holding your equipment on your cart while getting to your spot.
- Bait board: At least fourteen inches by fourteen inches, to cut bait. You'll also need a slot to keep your bait knife and a taped hole for rigs.
- Fixed rod holders: For safely securing your rods while baiting up rigs and storage.
- Hook/rig holder: Added on to keep extra rigs hooked up and ready for action.

I prefer a beach cart with a backboard so that I can hang tackle or clip on a nightlight to illuminate my workspace. Most bait boards are wooden, so you should reseal them once a year with polyurethane. I suggest that you invest in an external hauling tray for your coolers and your beach cart. These carts take up a lot of room and are covered with sand. These will slide into your trailer hitch receiver and are very useful for other purposes as well. Most local auto parts' stores carry these. Don't forget to rinse off your cart with fresh water after each visit to the beach.

One of the many advantages of living in the South is our Indian summers. An Indian summer is one in which the warm summer temperatures continue into the early weeks of the fall. Over the past two decades, these summer-type temperatures have been reaching further into the fall. Usually, I can be spotted wearing shorts and a light sweatshirt well into December. The coastal water temperature usually remains fairly bearable around the mid-sixty-degree mark. Most people are able to withstand this pretty well. Your feet will moderate to this water and stay warm. In fact, I usually do not get a chill until the sun goes down.

The anglers who use four-wheel-drive SUVs have it made. They can carry virtually the kitchen sink. It will only take you one or two trips hiking with gear to the beach to get the point. Not living at the coast, I really like to maximize my time actually fishing. I tend to go to the beach for the entire day for several reasons. I do not want to miss any potential action. When fishing without the luxury of an SUV, having a few buddies with you works well. You do not want to leave your gear unattended at anytime. Having a buddy watch your gear is not the same as having your line tended. The rulebook clearly states: any line left unattended in the water that gets a strike and is reeled in is awarded to the angler reeling in the fish. The rulebook further states that the owner, and only the owner, is responsible for any lost rigs or outfits left unattended. Here is one scenario that I can attest to: Our group is on the beach, set up with lines wet. One or two of the guys head to the beach house to partake in snacks and libations. A blitz comes on real fast; within thirty seconds, every baited line in the water is "fish on." The reel drags are screaming. The rods are flexing. You try to gain control and set both of your outfits as a school of chopper bluefish run up the beach. What to do? Well, at best you can secure any unattended gear from being pulled into the ocean. Short of cutting the line (his, not yours), you will not have time to do anything else. I have seen this happen only twice. I was able to rescue all the gear but was able to land only one of my fish. Two lines were cut by the fish, while a third slipped off the hook. Fishermen who repeatedly leave their lines unattended are not considered serious anglers. They are often left off the invite list after repeated violations.

Chapter 7

Protecting and Maintaining Your Gear

Every piece of your tackle that makes its way to the beach must be cleaned. Rinse your rods and reels with fresh water at the conclusion of each day of fishing. Pay close attention to the eyelets and reel seats when cleaning your rod. Rinse your reels with fresh water from the tap. Do not spray with a nozzle, as this can force water into the reel interior and cause failure. Never submerge your reels under water. Do submerge your rigs and lures to facilitate removal of sand and salt water. Allow all tackle to dry completely prior to storage. Wipe down your rods and reels with a polish cloth to remove any residual mineral deposits left after rinsing.

I am of the opinion that every moving part of your reel should be oiled. This should only be applied when you return home and have completed the wipe-down and polish procedures. Go sparingly when you apply oil. Only a drop or two is needed. Wipe away the excess, and never let any oil get on your line. I suggest using binding lubricant such as "red hot oil." Avoid using aerosol spray oils such as WD-40.

Make certain that you loosen the drag on your reels before storage. Backing off on the drag will prevent the washers from becoming compressed. If these washers become compressed or flat, your drag will not function as intended. Be sure that your hands are clean and free from oil and other contaminates such as hand sanitizer prior to handling your gear. The slightest scent from a strong harsh chemical material on your rigs or bait will drive the fish away. After I return home from each expedition, I wipe down each rod and reel with a slightly damp sponge or cotton wash towel. Make certain that you always soak and rinse your lures in fresh water after each and every use. Lures designed for fresh water will show signs of corrosion within a day if not properly taken care of. If a rig or lure is showing any signs of rust, do not re-introduce it back into your tackle box, as it can cause rust to other equipment it comes in contact with. Instead, wrap it in aluminum foil and discard it in a trash receptacle. Make sure that you clean every inch of your rods, especially in and around each of the eyelets. Mild soap is helpful. The eyelets will collect seaweed and other debris that will dry and harden; this can damage your line as it passes through the guides. At least once a year, I use a two- by two-inch piece of fine-grade emery cloth on the connections where my rods join. Very carefully, use this small piece of emery cloth to rub the male end of the rod connection. This will ensure that your rod will come apart upon request. Do not turn or twist your rod ends apart with the eyelets. Do not allow your eyelets to be used for any type of grip.

COOLER REQUIREMENTS

BAIT KEEPERS: Keep your bait separate from your catch, drinks and snacks. I keep my bait in a collapsible, zip-up cooler (six-pack size) that I keep inside of my large bounty cooler for ease of travel.

BOUNTY COOLERS: The average-size cooler for keeping your fish freshly iced is the thirty- to forty-gallon model. Rarely will you be landing huge fish that you will want to keep. Most of the fish that you will keep for consumption will easily fit within a thirty- or forty-gallon cooler. Make certain that you have a sufficient amount of ice to keep everything cold during your outing.

REFRESHMENT STORAGE: Keep it light. Put your bottled water and snacks inside a jumbo Ziploc type of baggie inside your bounty cooler, and keep it tightly sealed. Snack crackers, beef jerky and other foods can easily absorb a fishy taste. Do not over pack. Take a few packs of Lance crackers or maybe some fruit and a few bottles of chilled water. Do not take heavy/greasy foods, as they are messy and not well suited for consumption in the sand. Greasy foods (chicken, beef, etc.) will get all over your gear and your hands and can lead to problems. Don't waste your time and energy hauling a bunch of alcohol to the waterfront. Be careful not to handle your bait or rigs with any residual oils or lotion. The scent can keep potential aquatic suitors away from your offerings.

Use a magic marker to mark legal species slot sizes on your bounty cooler for quick access. You want to release any undersized fish quickly to ensure their survival. Further, if you are in the midst of a blitz, you do not want to waste time pulling out a tape to measure your quarry. Do not consider keeping or getting caught with any illegal-sized fish. Possession of any regulated species of fish with its head or tail removed will cost you a fortune and will ruin your trip. Wildlife enforcement officers will afford you no leniency for this violation. It is very illegal to possess *any* regulated species of fish with its head or tail removed. Do not risk cutting up any regulated species of fish as bait. Note that any law enforcement agency may inspect the contents of your cooler at any time.

Always wash your cooler with warm soapy water after you get home from the beach. Make sure that you dry your cooler and let it sit in the sun with the lid open. Only after your cooler is bone dry is it safe to store with the lid closed until next time. Note: Please make sure that your cooler's drain plug is closed tightly before attempting to put it in your car. I helped my neighbor pay for a new carpet pad for his new SUV after a soaking with gamey water.

Chapter 8

Species Identification

The game fish we faithfully pursue are always the consummate predators. One of the most basic requirements in becoming a seasoned angler is having the ability to quickly and positively identify the majority of fish species. Learning the name and family of each saltwater fish takes time and patience. You can learn how to identify the most popular species from photos and diagrams. Another way is to visit your local seafood market and closely look at the specimens for sale. Pay attention to the overall shape, coloration and markings that differentiate the species from one another. When we consume fish meat, we are actually feasting on the fish's muscle. Fish are coldblooded vertebrates. Fish scales act as a protective armor and are arranged in a pattern much like roofing shingles on a house. Fish are covered in a mucus coating that prevents dehydration and helps ward off infection. Care should be given not to remove this slimy coating when handling a fish for release. All species of fish must regulate their bodies' salinity—that is, the level of salt water in which they must exist in order to survive. Fish must balance the level of salinity to that of near equal parts between salt water and fresh water. This vital function is regulated through the process of osmosis. Some species of fish continue to grow; they do not cease growing until they die, as they do not reach maturity in growth as other animals do. Fish have both paired and un-paired fins. The paired fins are those that are evenly matched on both sides. Un-paired fins are those that are on the top, bottom and tail of the fish. Paired fins are the pectoral and pelvic fins and are used primarily for turning. The un-paired fins include the dorsal, anal and caudal fins, which provide propulsion. All fish species illustrations are courtesy of Duane Raver Jr.

BLUEFISH (*POMATOMUS SALTATRIX*)

Known commonly as "blues," this is a very popular surf species. They are silver in color with a blue-green tinge and have an elongated body with a large head and jaw, festooned with razor-sharp teeth. Probably the most voracious predator caught in the surf, they are unpredictable and spectacular game fish on the southeastern coast. To keep your bluefish as table fare, you must act quickly by bleeding and putting them on ice within the first few minutes to preserve sweet flavor. Bluefish must be bled at the moment of capture to preserve the sweet flavor. Otherwise, enzymes will release throughout the body quickly after being caught. Blues have a unique attribute that controls their mouths. Once a bluefish starts to close its mouth, it has to completely shut before it can reopen. This little feature, coupled with razor-sharp teeth, can and will lacerate your finger to the point of dismemberment. Never put your fingers near the mouth of a blue.

Bluefish are probably the most aggressive species of game fish on our coast. Bluefish travel in schools; thus, when you catch one, you will probably catch more. Blues appear to hit bait from any angle with no rhyme or reason. They tend to attack almost simultaneously, causing commotion. Stripers and trout tend to patrol the surface in a similar fashion, causing a big ruckus. As the species grow larger in size and weight, they tend to travel

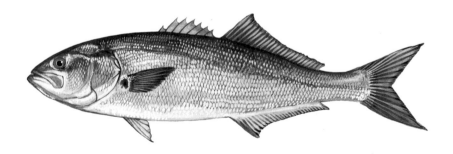

in smaller schools. As a species, blues tend to travel together with similar-sized bluefish to avoid being eaten by their larger cousins. When the blues approach ten pounds, they are called chopper blues. Deploying a metallic/red-colored lure will serve you very well in pursuit of these monsters. One of the most effective lures for this is the large Hopkins spoon affixed with a single hook. Try a double fireball rig armed with 1/0 to 4/0 long-shank hooks with fresh and juicy cut bait. When they start to blitz, they will literally swim through the water with their mouths open through a school of baitfish. It is common for schools of baitfish to intentionally beach themselves during a bluefish run to avoid the carnage.

The younger blues, weighing in at less than one pound, are referred to as snappers. The next category is called tailor blues, which are in the one- to three-pound range.

More often than not, you can catch flounder and red drum hovering under a school of feeding bluefish, picking up the leftovers. Casting a metal spoon into the heavy rolling surf is prime. Bluefish cannot rest stationary in the water, as can many other species, since forward motion is required to keep water flowing over their gills. The same is true for the freshwater catfish. If you are fortunate enough to see the pelicans diving after mullet, chances are they are being forced up from the depths by sizable blues. The current International Game Fish Association (IGFA) record is thirty-one pounds, twelve ounces, taken off Cape Hatteras. Blues prefer the water temperature between sixty-five and seventy-four degrees.

COOKING GUIDE—meat texture: fat; best preparation method: baked, second broiled; flavor: good.
Note: Eat fresh only, bled and iced within minutes of catching.

RED DRUM (*SCIAENOPS OCELLATUS*)

Also known as puppy drum, redfish and channel bass, this is a highly prized and regulated species. There are very strict limits on numbers and size. Red drum are widely considered the most sought after of all species caught from the surf on the southeastern Atlantic coast. Red drum can be distinguished from their black drum cousins by their lack of chin barbels and more elongated body. The body has coppery overtones on a silvery gray background. Lastly, all reds sport a large black spot about the size of the eye on either side of the caudal peduncle at the base of the tail fin.

Occasionally, there are multiple spots located on the upper flanks of the species as well.

As the tide rolls out, drum will tend to congregate at the back end of the sloughs, where they wait for an easy meal of baitfish being washed past the slough. Successful spawning seasons are sporadic; thus, it is vital that each female be able to produce several seasons of young. Reds will readily take a surface plug presented in shallow water. Do not think that redfish are purely bottom feeders. Many quality keepers can be caught hitting a top-water plug intended for weakfish. If you are using a surface plug to go after a red, chances are that you will land one on the larger size of the slot. Larger specimens tend to be coarse and stringy and not very palatable. As a rule, smaller puppy drum do not pursue top-water offerings. All members of the drum family are opportunistic. When drum are feeding on abundant supplies of mullet, they tend to pursue from the bottom. Drum cannot resist crustaceans such as blue crabs broken into pieces. The red drum is a schooling species that occurs inshore over muddy and sandy bottoms.

When fishing the backwaters for drum, target the high-salinity mudflats and bays that are closest to the inlet. Large reds are taken from just above the breaker line on an incoming tide or near channels, inlets and shell beds. Smaller drum are caught closer to shore in the sloughs, especially during high tide. This is a good time to present your surface plug in hopes that a trophy red will bypass the school for your plug. The fish will hone in on the lure's vibration and the silhouette when being drawn to the surface. More red drum are caught and released than kept as table fare. Large bull reds can be brutal on artificial lures and their hardware.

Locating red drum is made easier when they are compacted in large numbers in somewhat clear and shallow water. Their coppery color is easily reflected by the sunlight and projects a distinct brass-colored patch that will appear on the surface of the water. There are two ways to catch red drum. Many anglers let the fish make a run before taking in the slack and power setting the hook. Most anglers set the hook almost immediately to eliminate allowing the drum to spit the hook after sampling. This species has the keenest sense of smell of all fish caught in the surf. They will go after what is most plentiful at feeding time. More often than not, a drum will pick up your bait and swim toward the shore. Your reel won't scream, and your rod will not double over. Instead, your line will go slack and your rod tip will go straight. When this happens, deliberately pick up your rod, reel in the extra line and pull back very hard. Drum are very aggressive fighters that will afford plenty of action for the most seasoned angler. The IGFA World Record was caught at Avon, North Carolina, weighing in at ninety-four pounds, two ounces.

COOKING GUIDE—meat texture: lean; best preparation method: baked, second steamed; flavor: very good.

BLACK DRUM (*POGONIAS CROMIS*)

Black drum are a very popular species that inhabit nearly every inshore area. Most are pulled in around structures such as bridge and pier pilings. Many are caught close in the surf over sandy bottoms. The black drum is easily distinguished from the red drum in that its shape is shorter. Black Drum also sport very large teeth, which are used to crush shellfish and mollusks. Unlike red drum, they possess several very sensitive chin barbels in which to locate food in the sand. Juvenile black drum have four or five broad, dark vertical bars on their bodies. These bars cause some anglers to confuse black drum with sheepshead. The species has multiple broad strips.

The drum family of fish is so named for the drumming sound that resonates from their air bladder. This drumming is associated with the spawning season and probably assists in locating and attracting mates. The drumming of the males is particularly loud as compared to the softer sound generated by the females. Both red and black drum have been known to live for as long as sixty years. Small/juveniles weigh from four to ten pounds and are the perfect size for table fare. The larger sizes of the species run

from fifteen to twenty-five pounds. Smaller drum are much more flavorful than their larger cousins. The best places to locate the species inshore are in and around jetties, pilings and piers. The species is sluggish and does not strike quickly or with a great deal of force. They will put up a tough fight when engaged. Black drum will eagerly take live shrimp suspended beneath a float during the summer months. The species is not subject to bag or creel limits. Chartreuse, yellow, green or white grubs or lead jig heads, smaller inlets and creeks tend to warm up earlier than the larger bodies of water.

BAIT—shrimp, clams, crabs and artificial buck tail lead heads.
COOKING GUIDE—same as red drum. Flavor: good.

FLOUNDER (*PARALICHTHYS LETHOSTIGMA*)

Also known as fluke north of the Mason-Dixon line, flounder can be caught with live minnows, shrimp and sand fleas. Flounder begin life swimming upright, as do any other fish. They start off evenly balanced with their eyes on opposite sides of their heads. However, as they begin to mature, the species begin listing to one side. Which side they list to is dependent on their exact species. Summer flounder are a left-eyed species. Gradually, one eye will slowly migrate to the fish's "top" side. At this point, it permanently swims sideways and remains in a flat posture.

This flat feature affords the flounder the ability to become an excellent predator. It will bury itself in the sand as it waits to ambush unsuspecting prey. The underside of the flounder is a white smooth skin that is excellent bait when cut into strips. Due to long-term over-fishing, they have been depleted. The species is rebounding with the aid of harvesting regulations. Most flounder are taken off the bottom, sometimes in as little as six inches of water. Allowing your bait to move freely along the bottom will generate more strikes since drifting covers more area and keeps the bait or lure in motion. The largest fish are caught late in the season. Deploying cut or live bait will produce the highest yield of fish. Baiting up with live minnows is usually the most productive. Fluke are smart. They usually attack prey (bait) in two bites. The first bite is to sample the bait. The second bite is to swallow. When you first detect a strike, afford some slack in your line. This will help ensure that the fish is not spooked by any resistance. When you feel the second hit, set the hook firmly. Two of my favorite rigs for the species are the fluke killer and flounder pounder. The majority of flounder are caught in depths of five feet or less. Jigging with a chartreuse tipped with a fingernail-size piece of shrimp will bring on the fluke. We are fortunate to have not one but two species of flounder, summer and Atlantic. Summer flounder are identified as having multiple yet distinct oscillated spots on their brown topside. Atlantic flounder is black on top with white spots and prefers lower salinity.

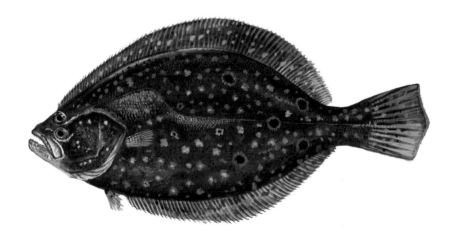

Flounder are relentless predators. They are very opportunistic feeders when the dinner bell rings. They are smart to the point of being easily spooked. Given a choice, they will congregate around structures waiting for easy offerings. Flounder will hold their ground while foraging for a meal. They tend not to be very mobile, instead waiting for the unsuspecting baitfish to pay a visit. The age-old modus operandi for flounder is to lie in wait. They seldom forage to find food, preferring to take advantage of their natural camouflage and exploit opportunities that come their way.

It is important to keep your bait moving. This can be accomplished through drifting with the current or slowly retrieving your rig. The best bait used to catch flounder is fresh shrimp and live minnows. Consider trying darker belly strips when the water is very clear. Flounder rely very much on sight feeding. Generally speaking, they need to see the bait or they do not strike. Use chartreuse, white or silver spinning blades with a baited buck tail hook for the most productive presentation. When retrieving your bait, keep your rod tip level with the water to keep your hook close to the bottom. Smaller inlets and creeks tend to warm up earlier than the larger bodies of water. Catch the beginning of a late afternoon ebb tide during the early spring for flounder. Carolina rigs baited up with live minnows work exceedingly well.

I have had more success landing fluke when the water is calm and flat. They will bury themselves in the sand and wait to ambush a passing meal. You want to deploy a smooth, flat, coin-like sinker that will glide across the bottom. Doing this with a natural strip of bait can be very rewarding. Flounders tend to sample their lunch first, and then they will pick up the bait for a taste, hold it and then swallow the hook. Afford yourself a two- or three-second count before setting the hook to ensure proper capture.

Flounder gigging is part of our southern culture. A night when the winds are still is best. Be careful not to mistake a stingray as a flounder. Use a lighted headlamp, a stout gigging tool and protective footwear. In less than one foot of water, look for eye movement and a convex outline in the sand.

COOKING GUIDE—meat texture: lean; best preparation method: fried, second broiled; flavor: excellent.

MENHADEN (*BREVOORTIA TYRANNUS*)

Commonly called bunker or porgy, menhaden are used primarily for bait. They are very oily and unpalatable for human consumption. Menhaden are a popular commercial ingredient within the cosmetic and agricultural industries. Their appearance is dark on top with a silvery color underneath. Menhaden travel in large schools and are commonly caught up to ten inches in length. They provide an important food source for numerous other pelagic species and are excellent bait for fishermen. In fact, menhaden are probably the most important baitfish on the eastern seaboard. This oily meat will attract scavengers as well as stripers, specs and blues. The only practical way to catch this bait is to use a seine. Menhaden is used in great quantities as chum for deep-sea fishing expeditions. Bunker is most effective when it is cut into smaller pieces. Menhaden should be kept very fresh. Do not allow to freeze or else the meat will become soft and will not hold a hook. Do not attempt to scale menhaden, as this will further weaken the fragile skin. Menhaden will spoil quickly and must be kept on ice until ready to use.

COOKING GUIDE—don't waste your time.

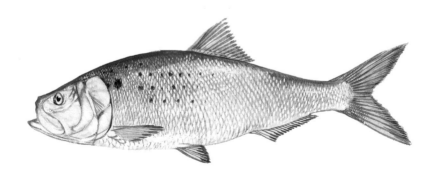

SPECKLED TROUT (*CYNOSCION NEBULOSUS*)

One of the most beautiful yet voracious species along the eastern seaboard, speckled trout, aka "specs", are among the most popular and pursued species. Specs are coveted and revered among saltwater enthusiasts. They have very soft mouths that hooks can easily tear if you attempt to lift a trout out of the water by the hook. Trout are usually more aggressive early in the morning or later in the afternoon, as they seem to have an affinity to lower levels of light. The most productive months for the species are early spring through late April. Specs feed voraciously during spawning season. Speckled trout are among the most finicky of species. They are one of the few species that are considered to be more residential, not migrating too far from their home spawning waters. Speckled trout are very prolific spawners. Specs make for most delectable table fare. Trout are among the most plentiful and prolific fish in the world. Unlike most species, which spawn once per year, specs can reproduce with great frequency. They sport two large recurvate canine-like teeth in the front of the upper jaw. There are numerous round dark spots on the back and upper flanks, as well as on the tail and rear dorsal fin. The large bull females will hold up in the shallow flats as they prepare to lay their eggs. Trout breed in the warm shallow waters, kept warmer from the sun. As a rule, the females are larger than the males. Casting an artificial shrimp affixed to a lead jig head will suffice just fine. Tip it with a

piece of fresh shrimp the size of your fingernail for a hint of flavorful scent. If you want to avoid having to refresh your bait every other cast, consider a synthetic. When the shrimp are abundant, the trout should be plentiful, as they will feed on them almost exclusively. When working a lure, a slow retrieve is critical. Falling tide in the early morning is very productive. Specs have excellent eyesight. Tie your lure directly to your line for best results. Specs rate very high as table fare. They tend to spoil rapidly unless covered in ice as soon as captured. Spotted sea trout are one of the few species that depend on estuaries throughout their life cycle. Specs often stun baitfish with their razor-sharp teeth prior to consumption. Patient anglers let them eat before setting the hook.

Many anglers report that fishing with live shrimp has salvaged many a summer day's trout fishing using a float/bobber in shallow water. This method is most productive once the current starts to recede.

Cooking Guide—meat texture: lean; best preparation method: broiled, second baked; flavor: excellent.

Gray Trout (*Cynoscion regalis*)

Also known as weakfish, a close cousin to the speckled trout, they have very soft mouth tissue that is easily torn during the retrieve or when trying to lift the fish out of the water by using your line. Both species of trout are more often pursued using artificial lures and baits. Weakfish are some of the best-tasting fish you will ever encounter. Their bones are

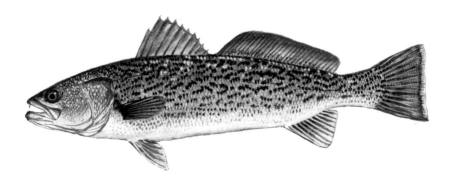

few and soft, so there is no point in filleting them. They are fat enough to smoke or broil and are excellent table fare. Gray trout feed on squid, shrimp and fish or any other bait that presents itself. Their front teeth are excellent, razor-sharp weapons that can dissect almost anything. Like their speckled cousins, they sport two large, recurvant canine teeth in the front of the upper jaw. The lower jaw of the species projects noticeably beyond the upper jaw. Many times, anglers fishing for flounder will catch them while using strips of squid. They are caught from April through early fall in sloughs and in channels. Gray trout mate in the back bays where the water is of a high salinity value. The eggs hatch within a week and grow rapidly. The average life span is usually three to five years. They grow to an average weight of just less than two pounds and fifteen inches long. The larger fish of the species are always the females. Be mindful when reeling these fish in and removing from the water, as your hook can easily tear through the soft mouth, hence the name "weakfish." Their meat is tender and white, with a high moisture content. The skin is usually left on during cooking to hold the meat together. Like all trout, the rich meat does not keep well and thus should be dressed and iced shortly after capture.

COOKING GUIDE—flavor: excellent.

BLACK SEA BASS (*CENTROPRISTIS STRIATA*)

This fish is excellent—highest-quality table fare! This is also a highly regulated species. Estuaries and sounds are prime locations to catch smaller ones called black Willies. They average one to three pounds. The 2012 size requirements require this species to be at least twelve inches in length in order to be kept. The majority of black sea bass tend to congregate in and around submerged structures such as pilings, wrecks and jetties. As the species increase in size, they move into shallow-shore habitats for the summer. They will retreat back into deeper water in the fall. As they mature, they will venture farther from shore each year. Every black bass that I have caught has been from bottom fishing. I have never seen the species being taken from top water. To the best of my knowledge, black sea bass are exclusively taken on natural baits. My favorite location to catch black sea bass is at Carolina Beach at the submerged remains of the

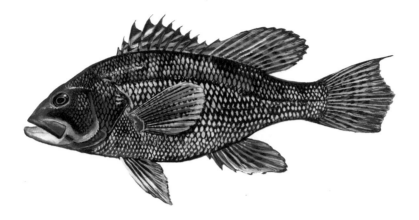

Civil War blockade runner about seventy-five yards offshore. Part of the remaining structure is visible at low tide. This species is among the first fish to spoil if not dressed promptly and packed in ice. If not gutted quickly, the liver will rupture and an acidic bile will spoil the meat.

BAIT—shrimp, squid, cut bait, bloodworms.
COOKING GUIDE—meat texture: fat; best preparation method: broiled, baked; flavor: excellent.

SPANISH MACKEREL (*SCOMBEROMORUS MACULATES*)

Spanish mackerel are one of the fastest-growing species of fish in the ocean. When you land a mackerel in the surf, chances are about 90 percent that you will have landed a Spanish mackerel rather than a king mackerel. The most productive time of the year to catch Spanish starts around the first week of April. Many anglers have a tendency to wait until later in the spring to pursue Spanish mackerel. The smaller yearling fish arrive about one month later. Of all the species of fish, Spanish mackerel tend to abide by the calendar more than any other species. The majority of our saltwater species tend to rely more on water temperature. Mackerel tend to forage in schools and travel in a pretty tight formation. They prefer water in the seventy-degree range or warmer. Thus, they migrate south when the water temperatures cool in the late fall. The majority of Spanish caught on the southern coast weigh about one to two pounds on average.

Fishing for Spanish from the surf usually requires a pretty long cast to reach the fish. Not too many are pulled in within a few yards of the beach. These torpedo-shaped racers will hit your lure like a freight train. I have had more success catching the species on small finger mullet. When I am fishing with artificial bait, I use gold castmasters or pink/white lead heads. The best natural baits for catching this species are live minnows hooked through the mouth or live shrimp suspended from a float. Make certain that you eliminate or minimize the use of any hardware such as swivels and wire leaders. Spanish have excellent vision and are easily spooked. This species is smaller than their king mackerel cousins. Both species of mackerel are identified by a blue topside and a silver underside and sport yellow spots. Spanish are extremely fast swimmers. Their forked, lunate tail and elongated body enable them to be among the fastest inshore fish on the coast. Spanish can best be distinguished from kings by the gradually sloping lateral line and the presence of bronze or yellow spots without stripes. Conversely, the king mackerel's lateral line shapes down sharply between the dorsal and anal fins. Spanish also sport eight unique finlets between the dorsal and caudal fins. It is best to fillet the smaller fish and steak cut the larger ones.

COOKING GUIDE—meat texture: fat; best preparation method: broiled, second baked; flavor: very good.

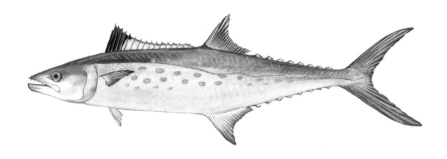

KING MACKEREL (*SCOMBEROMORUS CAVALLA*)

Kings are close cousins to Spanish mackerel. King mackerel are a coastal, pelagic, schooling species usually found in deeper offshore waters and thus do not venture so close to the shore that we consider them a major surf-fishing species. This is not to say that you will not get one in your cooler from time to time. Chances are ten to one that if you land a mackerel from the beach, it will be a Spanish. Kings are larger than their Spanish cousins. They become very aggressive when hooked and are known for their fighting ability. I have lost more than a few smaller croaker and whiting on retrieval due to aggressive kings taking a chunk of my fish as I reeled them in. King mackerel can be distinguished from their Spanish mackerel cousins by the sharp dip in the lateral line beneath the second dorsal fin. King have fewer spines in the first dorsal fin. Juveniles have spots much like their Spanish cousins, but they disappear with maturity. Like all species of mackerel, they grow fast and produce many young, which has enabled the species to remain strong and plentiful.

When a school of kings is spotted working baitfish off the beach, throw an artificial such as a gold Hopkins at them. The large king mackerel move toward the beach in late April and early May. When pursuing the breed with artificial lures, consider deploying a spoon or feathered jig head. The most productive natural baits are going to be live mullet or pinfish. Like all members of the family *Scomberomorus*, they must be dressed and iced as soon as they are landed to prevent spoilage. Their scales are much smaller than most every other pelagic species. Tradition has it that mackerel was the only fish sold on Sunday in fish markets of London, and it is the only

suitable salt-cured sushi. One of my favorite events in years past has been the annual Arthur Smith King Mackerel Tournament, an offshore event that traditionally produces citation-sized kings.

Every so often, you will be pulling in your fish and it happens—your line goes limp, but not in the same way as when your fish has shaken free of the hook. You will reel your fish up onto the beach only to see that it has already been cut in half. The bite will be so clean and perfect, bone and all. It is a beautiful sight in a disturbing way. You, my friend, will have been robbed by a king mackerel.

COOKING GUIDE—meat texture: fat/oily; best preparation method: broiled or baked; flavor: good.

WHITING/KINGFISH (*MENTICIRRHUS LITTORALIS*)

Also known as Virginia Mullet or Sea Mullet, this species is a member of the drum family. This species is very abundant and popular on the southeastern coast. Whiting are caught on shrimp, bloodworms or any other variation of cut bait. Whiting are bottom feeders and are most often caught with small pieces of cut bait with a simple bottom rig. They use their chin barbel to explore the ocean floor for shrimp and worms. The average kingfish weighs in at one and a half pounds and is long and slender in shape, usually up to one and a half feet long. They have been known to take lures that emulate finger mullet. Whiting frequent the shallow waters along our beaches. The species feeds most aggressively when the water is

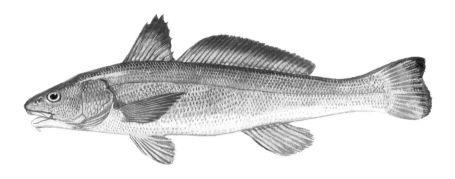

turbulent. The most common species caught in our waters is the southern kingfish. The species can be identified by eight dark diagonal strips on each side. The Gulf and northern species are somewhat darker in appearance than their southern cousins.

COOKING GUIDE—meat texture: lean; best preparation method: broiled, baked; flavor: good.

SPOT (*LEIOSTOMUS XANTHURUS*)

Spot (also part of the drum family) are one of the most common surf fish on the coast. Most anglers new to the sport will have plenty of fun getting into the spots. These delicious panfish usually travel in large schools. When the spot make a run on the pier or in the surf, plenty of excitement is guaranteed. It is more common to land two at a time during a run. Spot are one of the most abundant species in the Atlantic, in part because of their varied diet. Spot are one of the few intracoastal species that can tolerate a wide range of water temperatures and salinity levels. They are easy to catch, very abundant and make for good eating. Do not bother with attempting to fillet the species, as you will claim very little meat. Spot are very easy to identify by the small dark spot located behind the gill cover on the shoulder, hence

their name. Mature spot have a deep, short, compressed body with a short head and small mouth. Spot are easily caught deploying a single or double bottom rig. Small pieces of cut shrimp or bloodworm work very well. The species starts to move offshore in the early winter to breed. The spawning season extends from late fall to early spring.

BAIT—cut shrimp, bloodworms and minnows.
COOKING GUIDE—best preparation method: gutted and headed, fried whole; flavor: good.

PERCH (*BAIRDIELLA CHRYSURA*)

Atlantic perch are distinguished from spot because they have no dark spot located on their shoulder. Also, perch have a blunt squared caudal fin, unlike their cousins that have a deep forked tail. They are another favorite landed from piers and in the surf. The species is almost always taken while bottom fishing with a variety of natural bait. They usually weight in at about the one-half- to three-quarter-pound range. Reeling in a perch weighing over one pound is highly unusual. This is yet another popular member of the panfish family that makes for fairly good table fare. Panfish are so named

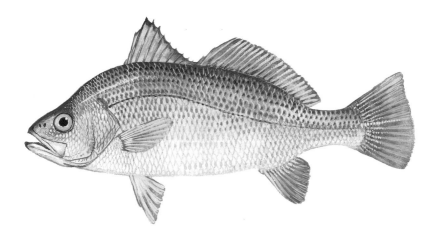

because they fit nicely into a frying pan when cooked. This species of fish is best prepared by gutting, scaling and frying whole.

COOKING GUIDE—flavor: good.

CROAKER (*MIRCOPOGON UNDULATES*)

Along with spots, croakers are members of the drum family. A favorite with young anglers, croakers are very abundant up and down the eastern seaboard. When the coastal waters cool down, croakers will move offshore until the return of spring. The species experiences problems when it enters the bay in late fall and winter. The cold weather kills many of the juveniles that are unable to adjust to the colder water in the backwater bays of the Chesapeake. Most of these younglings are going to weigh in at less than a pound and a half. Many of the juveniles fall victim to predators such as blues, stripers, speckled trout and fluke. Croakers live about nine years. Their coloration is a greenish-silver on top with white to yellow down below. The caudal fin is somewhat convex, as opposed to concaved like other species. The species is known for its very hard mouth that presents difficulty in setting hooks. These hard mouths make for an excellent tool in eating crustaceans. The species is caught regularly with shrimp and bloodworm. The record croaker weighs in at the four-pound-plus mark. Croaker flesh is very mild, fine grained and white when raw. The term "golden croaker" comes from the species' change in appearance, which

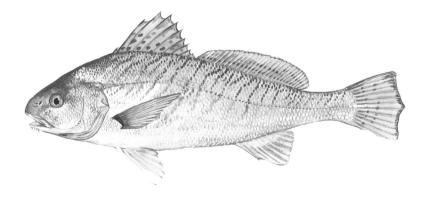

occurs during spawning season. Croakers are luminescent and appear pink when first removed from the water. A croaker's tail is slightly pointed, with faint stripes across its back.

COOKING GUIDE—meat texture: lean; best preparation method: deep-fried, extra crispy with tartar sauce and a squeeze of lemon; flavor: good.

POMPANO (*TRACHINOTUS CAROLINUS*)

Pompano love to feed on sand fleas (aka mole crabs). Pompano fishermen using double bottom hooks rigged with sand fleas have hauled in doubles while other anglers using shrimp or worm have looked on with envy. From September through November, you can land a nice-sized pompano in the one-and-a-half- to three-pound range. They put up a good fight and make for good table fare. The most productive rig for landing pompano is Andy Wright's tandem gold Kahle hook double bottom rig. Baited with sand fleas or clams in the right surf conditions, they can prove very productive. Optimal weather conditions for landing the species are when the barometer is changing and the water is clear. Fishing with light tackle is very productive when using one-and-a-half- or two-ounce sinkers tipped with fresh bait. Many times you will find pompano mixed in with smaller blues in pursuit of the same bait.

COOKING GUIDE—flavor: excellent.

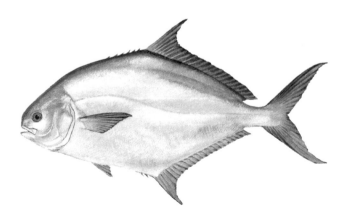

I felt compelled to include this delectable recipe for my favorite fish.

WHOLE ROASTED POMPANO WITH FENNEL AND BASIL
Yields 4 servings, total preparation time 30 minutes

rock salt
1 ½ pound cleaned/gutted pompano
1 tbs. kosher salt
1 tbs. cracked white pepper
1 medium lemon cut into ¼-inch slices
3 sprigs fresh thyme
2 tbs. extra virgin olive oil
1 medium orange
fennel and basil

Preheat oven to 400 degrees. Cover the bottom of a roasting pan with rock salt.
Cut fins and tail from your fish. Season cleaned belly cavity with salt and pepper. Stuff pompano with lemon and thyme. Drizzle with extra virgin olive oil.
Place fish on top of rock salt in previously prepared pan. Bake for 19 minutes.
Transfer fish to a serving platter. Dress with fennel, basil and a twist of sliced orange.

Bon Appétit!

STRIPED BASS (*MORONE SAXATILIS*)

Also known as Rockfish, stripers are caught both in fresh and salt water and are usually migratory. The species is easily recognized by the seven or eight black stripes on each side of its long, sleek silvery body. One strip runs along the lateral line, and the remainder are equally divided above and below the lateral line. Other members of the species remain non-migratory within estuarine river systems from Savannah to the

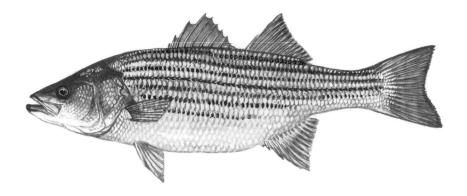

Chesapeake. Stripers feed most very aggressively when the water temperature is between fifty-five and sixty-five degrees. The species will feed when the water temperature falls below the fifty-five-degree threshold; however, they will go deeper in the water column to forage food. Striped bass are highly prized and strictly regulated. Effective fisheries management helped the species recover from severe depletion in the early 1980s to return to high abundance currently. The largest stripers are usually the females. Many are located in shallow waters and are most productive early in the morning with overcast skies. Striped bass prefer clear water and usually do not bite in muddy or cloudy water. The species is known to hold up around structures when tides are at their strongest. Many conservationists feel that nothing short of having the striper internationally designated as a game fish will ensure a recreational long-term striper fishery. The only other member of the bass family that comes close to fighting like a striper is the peacock bass of the Amazon in South America. I have fished for and caught both and prefer striped bass. The species rates very high as table fare.

BAIT—clams, whole finger mullet, bloodworms, cut bait.
FAVORITE LURES—plugs, buck tail jigs and spoons.
COOKING GUIDE—flavor: very good.

Cobia (*Rachycentron canadum*)

The cobia is the only known member of the family *Rachycentridae*. It has an elongated body with a broad and depressed head. The overall appearance is very similar to that of a small shark. In fact, cobias are known to congregate with sharks. The species' coloration and markings are quite distinctive. The top of the fish is dark mocha brown, while the sides are lighter with alternating horizontal stripes of bronze and white. The markings on the juveniles are much more pronounced. Cobia will hit your bait like a freight train. Count on long and powerful runs with the occasional leap out of the water. Many times, the entire school will break the water's surface in unison. A hooked cobia is a hard-running fish with lots of stamina and a bad attitude. This species must be subdued prior to close-quarter handling. The beasts can cause havoc for anglers. Many are caught on a king mackerel rig baited with live baitfish. The cobia population thinned out in the late 1970s and early '80s. The species rebounded in the 1990s. Most cobia landed in the surf will weigh in from ten to thirty pounds. As far as artificial baits go, cobia are caught using colorful, large (up to two-ounce) lead buck tail jigs. Cobia rate highly as table fare and can be prepared in a variety of ways.

Bait—porgies, crabs, squid and other fresh-cut baitfish.
Cooking Guide—flavor: very good.

SHEEPSHEAD (*ARCHOSARGUS PROBATOCEPHALUS*)

Sheepshead is an abundant species found along the southeastern Atlantic. The species is one of the most popular coldwater fish on the southeastern coast. They usually range from three to five pounds and travel in schools. The species is distinguished by its silvery-white torso. Sheepshead are very aggressive fighters and use their wide bodies as leverage. They can be caught on a variety of baits, such as shrimp, cut mullet or worms. They love small fiddler crabs and are taken with smaller hooks. They make very desirable table fare. These are my favorite cold-weather fish. Sheepshead are noticeably marked with six to seven vertical black stripes, which accounts for this nickname of "zebra fish." They are deep and compressed in shape, which affords them excellent leverage in a fight. They have a large head with massive frontal incisor teeth, which they use to chew open hard-shelled crustaceans and barnacles. Sheepshead can be somewhat of a challenge to catch due to their soft nibble that is not easily detected. The species is often located around underwater structures such as piers, jetties and bridge pilings. The average-size sheepshead landed on the southeastern coast weighs in the three- to five-pound range and is up to twelve inches in length. A fish weighing in at six pounds or greater is large for the region. They are non-migratory fish in that their only movements are from offshore to inshore for spawning. The fish is the namesake of a small bay outside Brooklyn, New York, where the species was once prevalent. Sheepshead have very lean meat and are excellent baked or broiled.

COOKING GUIDE—flavor: very good.

PINFISH (*LAGODON RHOBOIDES*)

This species of fish is known for being a nuisance more than anything else. Pinfish are the undisputed champions of stealing bait intended for other species. While some few are caught in the surf, most tend to prefer structures such as bridges and piers. However, pinfish are one of the best live baitfish used for catching large desired species. They hold up very well when rigged, hooked up and dispatched as bait. Pinfish are identified by the distinctive dark spot behind the gill cover and bright body markings that feature yellow fins. Pinfish will strike at most any cut bait but prefer shrimp and bloodworms. If you desire to catch these fish, use very small hooks and very little sinker weight. Pinfish do not make for good table fare due to their bony nature. The species is often used as bait or for chum.

COOKING GUIDE—flavor: nonexistent. Again, do not waste your time.

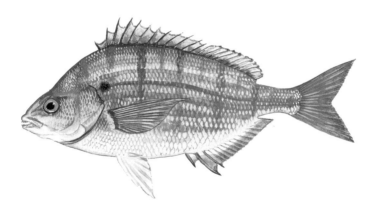

PERMIT (*TRACHINOTUS FALCATUS*)

Permit are a schooling fish that inhabit sandy flats and deep-water structures. The species is known to travel in schools of about ten fish or so. However, when they reach maturity, they tend to become more solitary. Permit are frequently confused with the similar-looking species pompano. They can be distinguished apart as the permit possesses fewer soft rays in the dorsal and anal fins. The body of the permit is laterally compressed, and the ribs are more prominent. Their coloration is silvery, with the back being a more

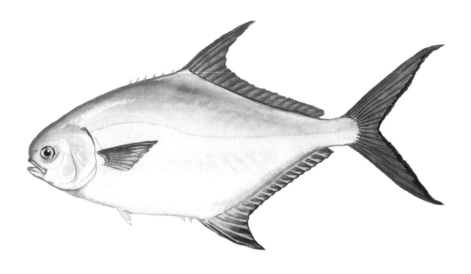

bluish-gray. The permit also has an unusual yellow triangular patch just above the anal fin. They use their flat bodies and forked tails as leverage during a fight and usually make a long, deep run when first hooked. Permit readily take crabs or shrimp and buck tail lead heads festooned with bright trimmings. Permit weighing from three to four pounds are excellent table fare. Most are taken off the coast of Florida.

COOKING GUIDE—flavor: good.

TARPON (*MEGALOPS ATLANTICUS*)

Tarpon was one of the first species of fish to be declared a game fish. This designation is earned and very well deserved. The species is found both inshore and offshore. Tarpon have the unusual ability to surface and intake air directly into the air bladder. This feature affords them the opportunity to inhabit brackish and stagnant waters that are virtually depleted of oxygen. These areas provide relatively safe havens from predators, thus offering a convenient refuge for the juveniles. They are covered with scales larger than almost any other inshore species. The tarpon sports a streamlined body, with the lower jaw protruding out and turned upward. The teeth are small, fine and well suited for successful foraging. Their coloration is a greenish-blue

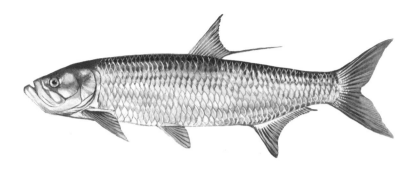

on the back. Their undersides are brilliant silver. Some of the species found within low-salinity brackish waters sport a golden color due to the presence of tannic acids. They mature slowly and will not reach maturity until they are almost eight years old. Tarpon are best caught at night fishing with live mullet. They are difficult to hook due to their hard, bony mouths. When hooked, hold on, as they will put forth a spectacular battle, often clearing the water when they surface.

COOKING GUIDE—flavor: fair.

SUCCULENT SHELLFISH AND CONSUMABLE CRUSTACEANS

Shrimp

Shrimp are the most popular seafood harvested from the ocean. They are caught by amateurs and commercial fishing trawlers alike. Bubba from *Forrest Gump* could rattle off some three dozen or so recipes for shrimp. I prefer them freshly boiled with hot and spicy horseradish-enriched cocktail sauce. Add a cold piña colada or other chilled fortified libation and you are good to go, perhaps with some circa 1970s tunes by Jimmy Buffett or Otis Redding to complete the ambience. Shrimp should be boiled briefly for no more than three minutes in rolling boiling water or until they reach a pinkish hue.

Blue Crabs (*Callinectes sapidus*)

The blue crab is the most popular edible crab on the southeastern U.S. coast. Crustaceans are the aquatic equivalent to insects here on land. They feed on microorganisms known as plankton. Blue crabs are the most abundant species of crab on the East Coast. They are among the most common species of crab that is harvested by commercial and amateur crabbers alike, and they make for very desirable table fare. In fact, all crustaceans and shellfish (shrimp, crabs and mussels) have very lean meat. Blue crabs are known for their delicious delicate white meat. Their name is a bit of a misnomer. They are actually olive green on most of their body, while the tips of their extremities are bright red. The male blue crabs are somewhat larger than the females. The underside of the male is marked by a sharply pointed ornamental apron. Conversely, the females' markings are more blunt and rounded. Blue crabs are excellent swimmers that can often evade predators. If speed does not aid in survival, the ability to lose a limb and grow a replacement can suffice.

INCIDENTAL CATCH

Skates, Rays and Jellyfish

You cannot control what takes your bait. No creature should lose its life for trying to eat to survive. Please carefully release any unwanted catch, such as sharks, rays and skates. They are a vital part of our ocean's ecosystem. Stingrays are usually not an aggressive species in nature. Their potent toxin is contained in a barb located at the base of the tail, not out on the tip. Some of the old-timers shuffle their feet when wading in water when they cannot see the bottom to avoid stepping on rays and skates. Unlike skates, rays can be dangerous to man. The species that is harmful is termed stingray. Aggressive medical attention is usually required if you are the unfortunate recipient of an encounter. Household vinegar applied to a jellyfish sting can neutralize the toxins, which can afford temporary relief.

Sharks

Sharks are beautiful fish with a full cartilaginous skeletal system and a streamlined body. They respire with the use of five to seven gill slits. Sharks possess a covering of dermal denticles that protects their skin from injury and water-borne parasites. This protective layer, combined with that streamlined body, greatly enhances their mobility. Sharks consistently lose and replace their teeth. The shark teeth we find on our beaches are fossils that are thousands of years old. The species is unquestionably at the apex of the pelagic food chain. They are the ocean's most misunderstood predators. Sadly, humans kill millions of sharks every year. When people retain shark meat for consumption, it rates very good as table fare. Shark meat is best prepared staked and grilled. Sharks should be bled, gutted and iced within minutes to preserve the taste. Blacktip and mako get the highest marks for food quality. Sharks mature slowly, produce few young and are victims of widespread overfishing. Demand for shark-fin soup in Asia drives extensive and sometimes illegal fishing worldwide. Many sharks are harvested for their fines only and then released to die on the ocean floor. I cringe when I see unwanted sharks, rays and skates that are tossed up on the beach and left to die. Some fishermen feel that they are justified and are doing everyone a favor by eliminating these species. This habit is a deplorable practice and should be discouraged at any opportunity.

Sea Turtles

The most well known species of pelagic turtles on the southeastern coast is the loggerhead. Loggerheads live in the open waters or in the estuaries. The female loggerheads lay their eggs in proximity to the sand dunes nearest the open beach. When the hatchlings emerge from their leathery eggs, they scurry down the beach toward the water. This yearly migration to the beach is met with much anticipation from environmentalists and predators alike. Seagulls and large horseshoe crabs await this abundant smorgasbord. They can grow to nearly five hundred pounds. The species is helpful to man in that they consume jellyfish.

Chapter 9

Inshore Fishing Techniques

Four factors that play more of a part in surf fishing than any others are:

- Food supply
- Tide
- Wind
- Water temperature

Reading the beach is the key to successful surf fishing. You must learn how to identify those characteristics that attract fish in the surf. Look for sand formations or any type of structure that will attract fish and bait. Find the bait and you will find the fish. Some features of the beach are obvious, while others are a little more subtle. The presence of food in the surf will often bring in the fish even if the other conditions are unfavorable. Beaches are constantly evolving. Sandbars and sloughs change with the weather and the current. The movement of baitfish very much depends on the temperature of the water and their own food supply. Each species of game fish has a temperature threshold that it prefers. Certain species of fish tend to congregate in certain levels within the water column. The feeding habits of baitfish can also coincide with daybreak. Most species of baitfish and game fish tend to rouse themselves as soon as food is available. This occurs at first light—not to be confused with sunrise. We have several different ways to determine if the food supply is readily available in the surf. About the easiest is to pay attention to the native bird species. Shore birds are most helpful. Seagulls will dive on baitfish that have been driven to the surface by predatory game fish. Poor baitfish can't seem to win. The birds are coming at them from the air, and game fish from the depths really leave these creatures doomed. When the game fish we are after force the baitfish to the surface, they are almost begging to be noticed.

Locating the slough in the surf is paramount to catching fish. The slough is an underwater feature, an elongated trough or depression that runs between the beach and the sandbar. Sloughs are present only when there is an outer sandbar. Thus, not all beaches have this feature. More often than not, you will be able to visibly locate the slough as it is exposed during low or ebb tide. Often, the slough will pool water that cannot recede over the outer sandbar. Search hard to locate the opening of the sandbar. This opening between the slough and the sandbar is where you want to fish. The waves will crest over the opening of the slough. Concentrate your efforts on the outside of the opening during an outgoing tide. Conversely, focus on the inside of the opening as the tide is coming in. Sandbars and inshore shoals can easily be identified as incoming swells move over them where the water piles up into breaking waves.

Game fish are most active during the last two hours of the incoming tide and the first two hours of the outgoing tide. Look for the most disturbed water, where the baitfish become disoriented by the turbulent water. After the fall bait run has past, most of our prized baitfish have retreated into the sounds, rivers and estuaries. You can find a few that linger close in to the inlets, which can produce some blues and kingfish.

It is not recommended that you wade past ankle deep into the water at night. Be careful not to turn your back on the surf. One rogue wave of four to five feet can knock you down. An important strategy for productive summer fishing is to be on the beach at sunrise. The clearer the water, the more important it is that the leader material remains invisible. The transition area between clear and dirty water usually holds generous limits of fish. Bigger fish typically feed most aggressively early in the morning on overcast days. They tend to retreat to deeper water off the beach toward late morning, out of reach of the surfcaster.

Jetties and breakwaters are similar to piers as they, too, extend into the ocean and offer a stable platform from which to fish. Most are constructed to protect marinas and inlets from the open ocean. Marinas and inlets require some degree of protection from the pounding waves and rough seas. Some are designed with a flat surface for ease of mobility. Others are not. Be very careful, as these surfaces become slick when wet. Be mindful of tidal changes so as not to be cut off with an incoming tide.

CONCEALED WEAPONRY

I do make at least some attempt to hide the hook in the bait. Do try to keep your terminal tackle as invisible as possible. Fish are not very smart. Large fish, however, did not grow large by being easily fooled. I do not like bringing any unwanted attention to my shiny hooks. I try to conceal as much of the hook point as possible when using natural bait. This serves a twofold point: first, the more contact the bait has with the hook, the better it will hold; second, shiny, metallic hooks are not indigenous to our waters, thus I do not flaunt them to my prospective quarry. Do not be overly concerned if your hook is not completely covered.

CASTING TECHNIQUES

Launching your rig from the beach out to the Gulf Stream is not always the objective. You need to be proficient enough to land your rig reasonably close to your target. Much of the coastline of the southern Atlantic is somewhat of a barrier island separated from the mainland by our Intracoastal Waterway. For the most part, this is a good thing. However, much of this coastline has a series of sandbars twenty to thirty yards offshore. Casting out this short of a distance will not present a problem during low tide. The challenge during high tide is that you will want to place your rig on either side of the sandbar. Placement of your rig will vary depending on a multitude of factors. Successful surf fishermen master both distance and accuracy. These two factors are dependent on understanding the variables. Taking into account the wind, the waves and the current will determine what type of cast to execute.

Almost always there will be a breeze or strong wind to deal with at the beach. With or without the wind, you must be able to cast your load to the desired spot in the surf. Here is my standard rule of thumb: I always start out using a rig weighted with three ounces of lead. If the wind redirects my rig, I will go to a four-ounce weight. If the four-ounce does not achieve the objective, I will go to a six- or eight-ounce rig. If this does not work, I consider going to the causeway. The same correlation may be applied fishing for large drum on the Outer Banks, where I start out with five ounces of weight.

Working a vertical structure such as a piling can be very productive. The goal is to allow your rig to drop to the bottom of the structure without swinging away and thus negating the desired effect. To achieve this result, cast as close as possible to your target. As soon as your bait or rig hits the surface, quickly afford your line some slack so as not to allow the tension of the bait's descent to pull away from the structure.

Casting your load to the desired spot is only part of the battle on a very windy day. Your fishing line will act as a sail on a boat! In turn, your weight or anchor will tend to roll along the surf until it is parallel with the beach. Not only does this result in slack line, but you will also not be able to detect a strike.

A trick that will help you gain an additional ten to fifteen yards is pointing your rod while rotating the tip the direction that your rig is traveling through the air. This technique reduces the friction from your rod eyelets, allowing your cast to travel farther. Another technique that will give you added control is feathering. Feathering gives you the ability to apply the brakes to your line. This course of action is used most often when you are casting around structures or controlling splash upon water impact.

Mastering the placement of your bait is of the utmost importance. Your rig or lure will travel in the direction your rod tip moved prior to it stopping. Accurate casting is one of the hardest skills of the sport to acquire. When I was a young boy growing up in Charlotte, I would practice casting in my front yard. I would tie on a two-ounce weight and cast to different spots in the yard. If you elect to use this technique, be mindful of windows, cars and people. Watch your rig and time your release on the backswing. Avoid snapping your rig at the start of your release. I have seen and heard of many rigs taking their final trips to Davy Jones's locker in this fashion.

In order to effectively maximize your casting load, you must begin the swing of the cast slowly. Quickly accelerate your rod in the desired direction to achieve maximum load prior to the point of release. If you begin the cast too fast, the rig will also accelerate too fast and not fully maximize the power of the rod blank. Your goal is to exploit the rod's fully loaded power. You must abruptly stop your rod without lowering the rod tip from the desired target direction. A fully loaded rod is one in which your rod is at maximum bend during the cast. This is referred to as "loaded" because you are committed to casting once in this position. Remember, your rod must be long enough to suspend your line above the breaking waves. This will help keep your rigs from being washed up to the shore's edge.

Exercise caution not to snap your cast to the point of losing your bait. Using the proper size and style of hook can help keep your bait on the rig. Use a slight rocking motion when getting set to load your rod. Time the

launch when the down swing of your load is extended. This will greatly reduce your chances of losing your bait or, worse, your entire rig during the cast. Make certain that your line is moving freely within the guides and is not wrapped around the tip before each and every cast. Failure to do so will break your rod tip and lose your load.

The basic overhead cast is best achieved when the rod is pulled in a forward motion in an upward arc while fully loading your rod. You must continually maintain the load until your release at the ten o'clock position. At the climax of the release of your load, your rod butt should be pulled to your hip while pushing the tip of the rod toward the ocean. Experience has proven that releasing your load at the ten o'clock position will afford you optimum trajectory.

When starting the cast, hold your rod in front of your body. Firmly hold the rod butt with your left hand while holding the reel seat with your right hand. Slowly move the rod back to the ten o'clock position, keeping pressure on the rig. Push the rod forward, creating the load. When your right hand moves to the front of your head, continue pushing forward while pulling backward with your left hand. Pushing with one hand while pulling with the other creates more power while increasing rod tip speed. Your goal is to have the rig enter the water just as the speed decelerates. The best trajectory for casting is when your rig hits the water.

To begin, spread your feet far enough apart to gain proper balance. Using your spinning rod, hold your right hand on the fore grip above the reel. Your index finger will hold the line while the bail is open. Place your left hand farther down the rod near the butt end. As the cast begins, the rod is brought up to a vertical position. Your right (casting) arm will push the rod's top section forward as the bottom hand is pulling the lower portion down. This motion must be smooth and powerful. At this point, pivot your shoulders and hips while shifting your body weight from the right to the left leg. This transfer of weight is instrumental in executing the proper cast. Only when the rod tip approaches the near vertical position of ten o'clock can you release your line, pointing in the direction of your choice.

If your rig enters the water too hard, the cast angle is too low. If the rig is dropping straight down, then your angle is too high. If the wind is to your back, consider a high lofting cast, as this will allow the wind to aid in deliverance. If you are casting into a headwind, consider using a sidearm that will aid in wind resistance.

When you are fishing in crowded conditions, stick with the overhead cast and use a shorter leader. Remember, you are responsible for your tackle! Be mindful of people walking behind you when you are casting. The basic overhead cast is the first cast that should be learned. Once this form is mastered, you can easily acquire more advanced styles of casting.

TYPES OF CASTS

People new to the sport of surf fishing often inquire as to why we have so many variations on casting. The reason is simple: different conditions require different approaches to casting. Fishing with an artificial requires a different cast from fishing with a drum rig or live bait. Practice and repetition will afford you improved proficiency with distance, power and accuracy. Improved shoulder rotation and body weight transfer will come with time. Proper leverage and power transfer will make your cast more fluid in motion.

Consider why tennis players and golfers use different swings when engaged in their sport. A golfer will strike the ball different from the tee box than when on the putting green. The tennis player will use a different swing when playing the baseline than when playing at the net. Different circumstances require different approaches to casting. Below are a few of the basic casting techniques that you will use when surf fishing. Each of the following offers advice as to which variation works best under which circumstance.

PROPER LINE FLIGHT: After releasing your load into the air, point your rod tip toward the outgoing rig as it sails through the air. This will reduce drag and friction from your rod increasing greater accuracy.

OVERHEAD/CONVENTIONAL: The traditional cast in which the rod is loaded while pulling your rig from your back to your front. This is the easiest cast to learn and use. Fishing in a strong wind is difficult. Casting at any direction other than into the wind allows your line to act as a sail and greatly reduces your distance. Try casting overhead with a very low trajectory into the wind. With a little practice, proper execution of this technique will allow you to cast sixty to eighty yards consistently. If this does not work, your conditions will improve at sunset when the wind moderates. The overhead cast is best achieved when the rod is pulled in a forward motion in an upward arc while loading the rod to maximum power. You must continually maintain the pressure of your load until you release at the ten o'clock position. Releasing at this position will allow you to achieve optimum trajectory. In crowded conditions, use the overhead cast and a shorter leader to avoid accidents.

PENDULUM: Used primarily for launching the heaviest offloads into the surf. This cast takes a long time to master and is used with loads of ten ounces or more of weight.

SIDE ARM: This cast is excellent for casting a lure or light rig on days when the wind is strong. With practice, you will learn to cast your rig/lure only a few feet above the water's surface, thus reducing interference from the wind. Hold your rod in the vertical position to ensure that it travels near the surface.

FAN CAST: Casting in a manner that resembles the arms of a clock. This technique allows the angler to cover a lot of water.

BUGGY WHIP: Another light-tackle cast for casting a rig or lure that does not require fully loading the rod. The buggy whip is close to the swing used in tennis. This cast is a modified side arm cast in which the action is all in the wrist. This cast is only used when casting a lightweight lure or bait of less than one ounce.

MODIFIED PENDULUM: This cast is a variation between the overhead and pendulum in which the rod is only partially loaded on the release of the cast.

UNDERHAND CAST: This cast is used when fishing from piers and bridges. The rig is brought under the pier or bridge hanging approximately fourteen inches from the rod tip. Slowly, the rod is pulled forward, releasing the line in the desired direction. Make certain that you keep a firm grip on your rod when using this cast.

JIGGING TECHNIQUES

Selecting the correct weight for your jigs or lead heads is very important. If your jig is too light, the lure will have difficulty descending into the water. If your jig head is too heavy, you will lose sensitivity and feel. I am of the opinion that the correct weight for jig heads used along the southeastern Atlantic should be between one-quarter and three-quarters of an ounce. I incorporate two jig heads on one leader when pursuing specs. The preferred method is to cast out ten feet or so beyond where you think the fish may be. Let your rig settle to the bottom, and ever so slowly, lift your rod tip up to the eleven o'clock position and let it drift back down to the bottom. The majority of your strikes will occur as your rig is descending within the water column. When fishing this type of setup, you will want to use a slow-action rod, seven to eight feet with eight- to twelve-pound test with a fluorocarbon leader. After you hook your fish, hold your rod above your head so that your line stays clear of any submerged structures. If a sizable fish runs your line over a rock or piling, disaster is sure to follow. I have reeled in slack without the comforting resistance of a lure or fish on the end more times than I would like to admit. Yes, this is a line that has been severed.

You may on occasion want to heave a one- to two-ounce jig out to or past the second sandbar from the beach during low tide. Pull out your medium-action, nine- to ten-foot rod to reach this zone. This seemingly impenetrable water is a haven for sizable fish. If you are targeting sheepshead or black drum, you can encourage them to strike your jig if you tip your lure with a fingernail-size shrimp. If you are pursuing speckled trout or red drum, consider a Hopkins-style plug. This is very effective when jigged slowly near a structure. Jigging on the bottom with live or plastic shrimp with a popping cork is an excellent method of landing specs and fluke. "Free-lining" is fishing with little or no weight so that your bait can drift naturally with the current.

BOTTOM BOUNCING TECHNIQUE

A basic concept behind successful bottom fishing is mastering the ability to uncover structures that hold game fish. The most common form of structure that surf fishermen have is the naturally occurring depressions on the ocean's floor. A technique that I find most effective is "lift tipping." Tipping is an art form that consistently fills my cooler with fish. The technique works best when deploying a single or double bottom rig. After casting your rig out into the water, let it settle firmly into the sand. Your line should be taut. Normally, your rod is being held outward at about a sixty-degree angle toward the water. Very slowly, lift your rod tip upward by ten to twelve inches. You want to feel your rig tighten almost to the point of moving your weight. Raise your rod tip just short of displacing your weight. This slight action will move your baited hook just enough to garner some attention. The majority of your strikes will come as you lower your rod back to the sixty-degree angle. It seems that this movement is just enough to gain notoriety for your offerings. Countless times, I have fished side by side with other anglers using the same rigs and the same bait, and they bagel. (To bagel means not to catch any fish.)

Another variation of lift tipping is used when you are fishing in deeper water from a structure such as a pier, bridge or causeway. Keeping your rig taut, simply lift your weight off the bottom by three or four inches and let it drop. This produces the added effect of vibration and noise to help attract fish. Again, the majority of your strikes will come as your bait is descending to the bottom.

WHAT TO DO ONCE YOU HAVE DEPLOYED YOUR RIG INTO THE SURF: LYING IN WAIT

- Keep your line tight.
- Keep your finger on the line (many missed fish if not).
- Keep your rod tip up.
- Keep your bait and rig where you want it, not where the current takes it.
- Keep your line away from others' lines.
- Ensure that your sand spikes have not become dislodged.
- Keep your bait stowed.
- Watch the surf.

SETTING THE HOOK

Setting the hook refers to the method of forcing a hook into the fish's mouth. Most of the time, a simple snap of the rod is all that is required, provided the hook is sharp. Mastering this technique takes some time and practice. You want to ensure that you have full penetration into the fish's mouth, without jerking the rig or lure away with too much force. Saltwater species have different textures in regard to how hard their mouth is. Sheepshead and red drum have harder mouths than weakfish.

When you feel a strike, point your rod tip toward the direction of your bait. Quickly take up any extra slack and then pop your rod tip up and back to the twelve o'clock position. You will need to apply a strong, solid pull when attempting to set your hook. After you have set the hook, hold your rod close up across your torso. In order to better fight my fish, I press the rod butt firmly against my right hip while holding the forward grip with my right hand. This allows me to crank with my less dominant left hand. Keep your body weight shifted to your front leg while allowing your rear leg to act as a counterbalance in the sand. Setting the hook is at once the easiest and yet the most misunderstood action that a fisherman performs.

OPTIMUM ROD POSITION FOR MAXIMUM FIGHTING EFFICIENCY

When you hook a large fish, the amount of pressure generated by the angle of your rod is paramount to a successful landing. There are multiple positions and angles in which to position your rod while reeling in your fish. The most efficient angle is the 150-degree angle. This position allows the rod to bear most of the stress. This angle also puts the least amount of stress on your reel. Further, these positions afford the angler to sight the position of the line and follow the fish through the water. Some anglers hold their rods at the 30-degree position. This angle is the least effective and can damage the drag system on your reel. This position puts the majority of stress directly on your reel's mechanism. The 30-degree position does not afford your rod the opportunity to absorb the stress of the fight. The only time you should hold your rod in this position is when you are attempting to dislodge your rig from a snag. This position will prevent your rod from breaking under the extreme pressure of pulling your rig free. When executing this maneuver, wrap your line around your open hand five or six times. You will want to do this between the reel and the first eyelet. Certain occasions will dictate that you convert and retrieve at a lesser angle of 45 degrees. Consider going to this position when your fish is past the breakers and within ten feet or less from your feet. This angle will help ensure that your hook stays firmly secured in the fish's mouth. Avoid what is referred to as high sticking—when your rod is positioned close or near to the 180-degree angle. This position greatly reduces your leverage and can lead to a broken rod tip.

REELING IN YOUR FISH

The suspense thrills even the most experienced angler. Every time your rod shakes with action, you get goose bumps. None of us can deny it. We know in general terms what species we are pursuing, but you never quite know what has accepted your offerings. No matter what type of fish is on the end of your line, you will want to follow this basic protocol. Firmly, pick up your rod with both hands. Keep the rod pointed up while you thumb your drag. If your fish is large enough that he is stripping line while running deep, let him run. This will only wear him down.

Keep your thumb on the cylinder spool to act as a break. The more resistance your fish encounters, the sooner he will let you reel him in. Adjust your drag only after determining how much fight your quarry is putting up. Do not forget that your line being pulled through the water will also afford you some natural drag. Remember, the drag is to help ensure that your line does not break in the heat of battle. Assuming that your knots are good and your rigging sound, you should not lose many fish. Always keep your rod tip pointed up. Always keep your line tight—just tight enough to prevent any slack. This will help prevent your fish from shaking and dislodging your hook. Do not jerk on your rod, as this may tear your hook out of soft-mouthed species such as trout. Hold your ground; do not back up on the beach, as this will put you at a disadvantage when the fish hits the breakers. Let the incoming waves help you land your fish. Keeping your rod tip up and line tight, allow the waves to wash your fish up to you.

Use this time to spool in the excess line that is afforded you. When the wave is receding back out to sea, hold firm and pray. This is the point at which you are most likely to lose your fish. The force of the wave and the strength of your fish will test your resolve. Use those incoming waves to your advantage. Take up the excess line, keeping the line taut as you lower your rod tip from the twelve o'clock position to the ten o'clock position. Do not allow your rod tip to get horizontal with the water or below the nine o'clock position when reeling in your fish. Remember—use your rod to fight the fish, not your reel. Your reel is designed to take up the line not motor in your quarry. This is why we have nice fishing rods that are designed and rated to assist you in powering in your fish.

Keep that pressure constant when reeling in your fish. Several species of fish will run toward the beach and vigorously shake their heads in an attempt to dislodge your hook. When your fish is swimming toward the beach, you need to crank your reel as fast as you can to ensure that your line is kept taut. If the action is slow, I will leave two or so lines baited in the water while I work my way up the beach with a light outfit and an artificial. When I land something worth keeping, I will remain in that spot and continue casting. You can bury your freshly caught fish in the sand if you are not near your cooler. Make certain that you mark your location for retrieval. Your rod is designed for leverage and to bear the brunt of the fight. Pull with your rod and then crank in the slack with your reel. Remember, your rod tip should always be up. Use constant and firm pressure; never jerk or yank.

The key to successfully landing any large fish is to simply remain calm and allow the fish to tire itself out. When any species of large fish is hooked, it is going to take off. The initial run can strip your reel of one-hundred-plus yards of line in less than one minute. Do not try to prevent your fish from running. It is better to let the fish wear down than try to leverage him in with a fight. Do not pump your rod, as this action only reduces line slack, or the amount of line in the water. It is the drag of your line through the water that wears the fish down. You want your hooked quarry to run perpendicular to the beach. This forces the fish to move the line through the water, which, in turn, creates friction/drag. This is how many large fish are landed with seemingly light tackle.

Keeping your drag system set on a light setting will accommodate a long run, for which many large species are notorious. Remember that your line will create static drag from resistance with the water. Your goal is to close the distance between you and your citation-size quarry hooked on the other end of your line. Do not be lulled into a false sense of accomplishment when you start making progress. Large game fish always make a second run when they get close in to shore. When your fish has surrendered to your point of view, tread lightly, as there is a fine line between lifting and manhandling your fish out of the water.

When your fish is in sight, no more than a few feet out, firmly bend down on one knee and plant the butt of your rod in the sand, keeping the rod tip in the air. Reach out carefully to your prize. With wet hands, cautiously secure your fish to where you are able to remove the hook. Do not get so caught up in your catch that you let your rod fall over in the sand or water. If you do not plan to keep your fish, leave him in the water while you remove your hook. If need be, deploy your pliers to aid in hook extraction. Be careful; most every species of saltwater fish has extremely sharp teeth and would love nothing more than to lacerate you for your misdeeds. While we are on the fun topic of lacerations, I place a fabric Band-Aid on the third joint of my index finger prior to hitting the beach. Why? One time, I was attempting to adjust my drag while playing a large red drum. I was switching hands when my fish made a run. The joint of my finger ended up being sliced clean to the bone with braided line.

DECKING YOUR FISH...HOOK, LINE AND SINKER!

As soon as a hooked fish feels the hook, the fight is on. Most every species will make a run in order to set itself free. A hooked fish will try to shake or jump in order to lose a hook. Many species will make a long, deep run in order to get free. Seasoned anglers can often tell what type of fish they have hooked by the way in which the species will fight. A fish hooked in shallow water is much more likely to jump or act more frantically than a fish hooked in deeper water. As soon as you have your fish firmly hooked, you must maintain pressure on the line. If you afford a fish any slack in the line, it will detect the change and shake loose your hook. Some species will make a run straight at the beach, creating enough slack in the line to become free. You must have the ability to reel in your line very quickly to avoid this loss of tension in the line. Properly setting the drag can greatly help you maintain the correct amount of tension on your line. Fighting a larger fish requires a technique referred to as "pumping your rod." This is accomplished by quickly retrieving your line as you lower the rod until it is horizontal and pointed out toward the ocean. When your rod reaches the horizontal position, stop reeling in your line and slowly raise your rod up to near vertical. Repeat this process until the fish is near the beach and ready to be landed. Remember, never let the line go slack when reeling in your fish.

More fish are prone to be lost during the landing/beaching stage. When you are bringing your fish into the breaking waves, allow the waves to help surf your fish to you. Keep up that pressure and reel a little bit faster, as the waves will increase the speed with which your fish approaches your position. Make certain that you allow for enough play as the wave recedes and adds two or three times the amount of resistance as when the wave is coming in. Transitioning between maneuvering your rod while maintaining pressure and grabbing your fish is the most challenging. It is awkward, to say the least. If you are fishing solo, keep pressure on the fish first and foremost. Step into the surf just up to your ankles and drop down to one knee while planting your rod butt into your hip. Keep the rod in the vertical position while pressing the back of your reel seat firmly to your chest. Keeping your balance, reach out and pull the line double back to your rod. Grab hold of the line and hold it against the rod with the same hand. Immediately, with your free hand, net or grab your fish behind the gills and lift it out of the water. Be careful not to drag your fish up onto the beach through the sand unless you are certain that you are going to keep your catch.

High sticking: Avoid holding your fishing rod above the fore grip when fighting your fish. Fishing rods are designed to flex from the fore grip to the tip of the rod. Grabbing your rod above the fore grip can and will cause your rod to break under stress. When fighting a fish, keep your rod tip up and pointed in the direction of the fish. This will help you maintain the leverage to control the fight and will lead to a successful retrieval. Follow your fish rod up in the direction in the water in closest proximity to the action. Always keep your line tight so as not to allow the fish to shake lose your hook, especially right in close to the surf.

Keeping your bait moving slightly across the bottom will attract more fish. A light southeasterly breeze generates better fishing conditions. Deploy two rods, one with a mullet rig or heavy fish-finder rig out beyond the breakers for big drum or large blues and the second a light- to medium-class combination for close-in fluke, specs, croakers and other varieties. If the crabs are stealing your bait, use a small float to suspend your rig above the bottom. The lighter your line, the farther you will be able to cast, as there will be less wind resistance and reduced friction. Fish inside the slough at high tide if there is an outer sandbar present. Be careful not to overcast the fish, especially during high tide. Keep your bait fresh. Washed-out bait loses its scent and flavor.

Here are some other tips:

- An important strategy for productive summer fishing is to be on the beach at sunrise.
- The clearer the water, the more important it is that the leader have low visibility.
- The transition area between clear and dirty water holds higher populations of fish.
- Many types of spoons spin very quickly when retrieved, causing the line to twist and tangle.

- Bigger fish typically feed most aggressively early in the morning on overcast days. They tend to retreat to deeper water off the beach toward late morning, out of reach of the surfcaster.

HOOK EXTRACTION

This takes experience and patience—and a good pair of needle-nose pliers. Like the Japanese used to say when their cars were first introduced to the Americans, "It's better to push a car than to pull." The same is true when using your ever-improving skills of hook removal. Fishhooks are designed with a barb to catch and retain the fish until such time that we are ready to toss them into the cooler or release them back into the water. This barb is what makes hook removal tricky, as well as deadly to your fish. Many species of saltwater fish swallow the entire bait along with the hook. If you are not extremely careful when removing the hook, you can easily damage vital organs such as the fish's gills. If these are pulled and dislodged even slightly, you will end up with a floater. A floater is a fish that floats to the surface as it is dying. If a fish is having trouble getting and staying below the surface, it is doomed. As a last resort, use a wire needle to puncture the fish's bladder. The fish stands a much higher chance of survival if it can submerge below the water's surface. As a last resort, if you determine that you do not possess the surgical skills to safely remove said hook, simply cut away as much of the rig as possible. Continued exposure to salt water will cause the hook to rust in a week or so, and it will fall harmlessly out of the fish.

RELEASE TECHNIQUES

It is of the utmost importance that we do everything within our ability to ensure that we preserve all species of fish for future generations to enjoy. Only keep for table fare what you require. Fish that are released after being caught do survive to fight another day. When fish are fatigued or wounded from being reeled in, they release lactic acid proportionate to their physical stress. If the fish is able to restore its blood enzyme level to pre-stress levels within a few minutes of being landed, chances are that it will survive the encounter. The quicker you release, the better. Try to use as much caution as possible when handling any fish. To help ensure that your fish can be released successfully back into the ocean, retrieve and release quickly. Fish have a special slime type of film on their bodies that works as protection. Avoid removing your fish from the water if at all possible. Make sure that your hands are wet prior to handling your fish. When you release any fish back into the ocean, use caution and do not over-handle. Nor is it a good idea to drag your fish across the sandy beach. A fish is not a naval landing craft. Stress and wounding are very harmful aspects when landing a fish. If over-handled and not done properly, mortality will be the end result more often than not. Hook wounds to the stomach and gills are usually terminal. If you must handle your fish, slide your hand in the direction from head to tail. This will retract the spiny dorsal fins and save you from painful puncture wounds. If your fish does not swiftly beat a hasty retreat, he may be a bit overtraumatized. Never toss a fish back into the water; instead, gently release it by affording it the opportunity to gently swim out of your open hands. Try to revive your fish by gently holding it upright in the water, supporting the body from the underside, while slowly and deliberately moving it back and forth in the water. Be careful not to squeeze the fish. If you are so inclined as to take a picture, hold the fish by supporting its belly and hindquarters just shy of the fins. Make certain to keep your fingers out of the fish's gills.

Summarization of Tips for Safe Release of Fish

- Crimp the barb of the hook if you know in advance that you intend to release your catch.
- Never squeeze the fish or apply any amount of pressure while holding.
- Keep the fish in the water as much as possible.
- Do not drag the fish across the sand when reeling in your catch.
- Unhook and release the fish quickly.
- Avoid using treble hooks.
- Wet your hands prior to handling so as not to remove the fish's protective slime coating.
- Make certain to keep your hands and fingers out of the gills. This is critical to survival!

PELAGIC MIGRATORY PATTERNS

The migratory patterns of game fish are very parallel to that of the food supply. The migration of baitfish occurs only twice per year as the water temperature dictates. In the spring, as the water warms, menhaden, shad and silver mullet travel north. Conversely, the baitfish descend south in the fall as water temperatures cool. This annual migration affords those of us on the eastern seaboard an ever-abundant smorgasbord of fishing.

The huge schools of baitfish provide a feast for predator species such as drum, flounder and blues. We surfcasters count on these masses of baitfish to delivery our desired quarry of game fish. The bluefish follow the schools of baitfish, only to make a vicious attack through the school, chewing and chopping without mercy. Mullet are very fast-moving fish, while menhaden move more slowly in the tightly packed schools. Flounder and drum prowl under the feeding blues to pick up an easy meal with little or no effort.

Chapter 10

Preparing for a Successful Fishing Excursion

Surfcasting is a specialized form of fishing that demands advanced preparation and having the proper equipment. The main difficulty for planning a surf-fishing trip in the late fall is negotiating what to wear. Everyone tends to overpack for these beach excursions. We pack our thermals as well as our shorts, not knowing exactly what the weather will bring. I strongly suggest that you dress in layers, having the ability to add or shed extra clothes as the conditions change throughout the day. The biggest challenge to wearing or transporting these extra clothes goes to the foot-bound angler. He does not have the ability to pack everything for the haul to the beach.

I do not live at the coast. When I get the opportunity to go fishing, I want to hit the beach ready to go. I do not want to spend upward of thirty minutes tying rigs and getting organized. I find the time weeks in advance to get my gear and tackle ready for the trip. I pre-tie all of my rigs and have them sorted in Ziploc baggies ready to deploy. Usually within ten minutes of my choosing a venue on the beach, I have my first line baited and wet. Here are the basic rigs and tools that you should have in your arsenal ready to deploy after you get your chair out:

- 2 double-hook bottom rigs with a three- and four-ounce pyramid sinker; size 2 long shank hooks
- 2 single-hook drum rigs with circle hooks with a five-ounce sinker
- 3 fish-finder rigs

- 2 fireball bluefish rigs (one large diameter, one small diameter)
- 2 whole finger mullet rigs
- knife, pliers and hand towel on your belt

Have an assortment of lures and jigs ready to go at a moment's notice. If you witness a run starting up, you want to have your full arsenal ready to deploy. I usually keep a light tackle rod rigged up with a 1¼-ounce buck-tailed Hopkins spoon ready for action.

The first rig that I cast out is usually a double-hook bottom rig with #2 long shank hooks weighted with a three-ounce pyramid sinker. I will bait one hook with shrimp and the other with bloodworm. This is deployed first for several reasons: 1) I may catch a small enough spot or whiting to use as live bait for my large Hatteras Heaver; 2) I can get a general idea of what, if any, species are active; 3) I can monitor this rig while I am setting up my other rods and gear.

If within the first thirty minutes you are not getting any strikes, re-bait with something different. Most baits and lures used in saltwater fishing will attract many different species of fish. Many times, you can catch small puppy drum when you are pursuing sea trout. These two species have been known to be attracted to the same bait and lures of similar size. I am not a purist when it comes to surf fishing. I very much enjoy catching a mixed bag of fish. I bait my rigs to afford me this option. The closest thing to an exception would be when I deploy my heavy rod with a live baitfish. This rig is intended for a large something, be it cobia, large bull drum or big bluefish.

Chapter 11

Location, Location, Location

The eastern seaboard from the Chesapeake Bay to the Florida Keys is home to the best surf fishing in the world. Within this nearly 1,400 miles of pristine coastline is the most prized fishing venue on the globe. Unlike fishing a freshwater lake or stream, the open beach has little or no cover or structure in which fish like to take refuge. Fishing from an ocean pier does afford the angler the presence of pilings and shade from where presentation of bait is well received. Our fellow brethren of the coast who fish offshore have the distinct advantage of traveling great distances by boat to locate favorable hunting grounds. In addition to being mobile in a boat, one has the prime advantage of being fully equipped. We, the true surf fishermen, will choose a location on the beach in which to set up and patiently await our quarry.

VIRGINIA

I have always had exceptionally good fortune when fishing the Chesapeake Bay in Virginia, one of my favorite states. Fishing the bay in the spring and fall will prove to be most productive when chasing red drum, chopper blues and cobia. The prime season begins in early April and climaxes in late June. The climate begins to change in September, driving the large drum out of the bay and into the open ocean. Local anglers prefer the eastern channel edge as the fish exit the bay. Anglers are allowed to keep up to three red drum per day that measure between eighteen and twenty-six inches. These are the perfect size for gourmet table fare. Cobia are a managed species as well. Each angler is afforded a bag limit of only one cobia each day. The minimum keeper size of the species is thirty-seven inches. This should not pose a problem, as the average size of the species will surpass this measurement. The Virginia state record for cobia is 110 pounds, taken at York Spit.

The Chesapeake Bay has more than two thousand miles of shoreline and is the largest estuary in the entire world. Despite its vast size, it is basically a shallow body of water. Fishing the Chesapeake is a treat. This is one of the most productive venues up and down the East Coast. Locate the rocky outcrops in water about twelve feet deep near the Flats or Gunpowder Shoals and deploy your offerings of fresh shad or cut bait menhaden. Artificial bait is not as productive, as these stripers can be rather selective in what they pursue. Small bay anchovies are one of the most predominant baits used within the bay. If you are in the mood for striped bass, consider heading back to the intracoastal rivers and tributaries. Speckled trout congregate in the tidal marshes along the edges of the grass banks as the spring winds drive them off the bay.

My preferred location to fish in Virginia is at the point on Hog Island. We have always been successful landing at least a few puppy drum and bluefish at this point. Lynn Haven Inlet near Norfolk has produced many large striped bass. Rudee Inlet at the southern end of Virginia Beach is most productive for catching flounder in the late summer on live minnows. The estuary at the Hampton Roads at the mouth of the James River is probably my second favorite venue in the Old Dominion State. The Chesapeake Bay Bridge-Tunnel (CBBT) is the longest bridge tunnel in the world at seventeen miles in length. The bridge is the most productive man-made fishing structure on the East Coast. The interior of the bay is suitable for small watercraft. The bay is least productive in the winter months, as fish migrate out to the open ocean. During very cold weather, nice fish can be located in the warm water where the power plant discharges at Calvert Cliffs near the Patuxent River on the eastern shore. Large, highly prized speckled trout and flounder hole up in these inland waters until late spring before moving offshore to cooler waters.

NORTH CAROLINA

Morehead City

Fort Macon State Park is one of my top five surf-fishing venues in North Carolina. The Rocks consistently produce excellent bounties of specs, blues and Spanish mackerel. Squid and live shrimp draw bites from nice red drum, while anglers hook up with bluefish and speckled trout while casting gold diamond jigs. The Atlantic Beach Causeway produces nice gray trout on green grub baits and Tsunami glass minnows. Anglers have good success with sheepshead in the deeper water beneath the railroad tracks while working stingsilvers. Spend some time at Beaufort Inlet and catch plenty of weakfish and Spanish mackerel. Plentiful numbers of flounder come from behind Shackleford Banks under the Atlantic Beach Bridge. Drifting with live mud minnows or finger mullet produces the most fish. Sheepshead are often caught around the pilings using fiddler crabs. Down to Salter Path along the Bogue Banks is excellent for speckled trout and flounder. Fort Macon has defended against pirates, Spanish and British naval insurgencies. In the Civil War, the fort was finally captured by the Union army and used as a prison.

Kure Beach

Fishing off the Kure Beach Pier is always exciting for decking spot, whiting and spadefish. The pier operators here are straightforward about what is running and what the fish are hitting. The surf heading due south of the pier seems to be more productive in the fall than the stretch north of the pier.

Fort Fisher

Fort Fisher is another Civil War–era military post. It is a state historical site located south of Wilmington down U.S. Highway 421. This is one of the region's most productive venues outside of the more publicized Outer Banks. Fishing for pompano off the rock jetties is productive in the summer months. In the surf, anglers have been hooking a mixed bag of puppy drum, whiting, spot and black drum. Parking is close at hand for easy in-and-out access.

Carolina Beach/Wilmington

Another one of the southernmost barrier islands, this is very reliable as a surf-fishing venue. Forget trying to fish between Memorial Day and Labor Day, as the crowds are overwhelming and the fishing is slack. Late fall and early spring are excellent for black drum and bluefish. Snow's Cut Inlet is excellent for flounder almost year round. Fishing for large sheepshead around the oyster rocks and other hard structures is solid using live fiddler crab. Carolina Beach State Park is an easy location to locate. Fishing off the banks here is hit or miss depending on what the weather is like. Another excellent location to fish in the area is at Masonboro Inlet and John's Creek. Check with the fine folks at Island Hardware, Tex's Tackle or the Intracoastal Angler for tackle and an update on what is being caught. Wilmington was once the largest city in North Carolina. The Cape Fear River winds through this deep-water port where the legendary battleship USS *North Carolina* is moored. Stroll along Wilmington's cobblestone streets and soak up the rich history.

Wrightsville Beach

This is one of my favorite locales for fishing. Generally, I catch a mixed bag between the months of October and December. April and May are also good months to fish cut baits up and down the beach, where a slough is always present. There are excellent runs of bluefish and drum in the late fall. Moving north of Johnny Mercer's Pier toward Shell Island, the beach flattens out to provide very little in the way of slope. You can wade out nearly fifty yards and be only knee deep in water. This insufficient slope is usually not as productive for surf fishing in the summer months. Go to the north end of Shell Island to the point between Figure Eight Island and Wrightsville Beach. This inlet holds excellent catches of sheepshead, fluke and puppy drum.

Bald Head Island

This is a restricted island for golf carts only. Fishing the northernmost point at the Cape Fear River Inlet is excellent for blues, drum and Spanish using the finger mullet rig. The tide line where the Cape Fear River discharges into the Atlantic at the north end of the island is the famous Point. The Point overlooks the notorious Frying Pan Shoals, where the water collides and the fish thrive. The ferry dock is another popular area to cast for specs at night under the lights using live minnows. Do not dismiss the tidal basin and the creeks on Bald Head Island. I have had excellent luck fishing these backwaters when the surf is too rough or the wind is too strong.

Oak Island, Ocean Isle and Sunset Beach

While these offer the most splendid beaches, this southeastern-most stretch of the North Carolina coast is mediocre at best for surf fishing. The primary reason is that these beaches have a southern exposure that offers very little slope. The shell flats on the back side of the island are usually the most productive location on the island. These calm beaches are the absolute best locations for families with small children.

The Outer Banks

Driving to the barrier islands known as the Outer Banks is a pilgrimage. Cross onto the barrier islands at Whalebone and head due south along Highway 12. Stop in at the Oregon Inlet Fishing Center for up-to-date fishing reports and supplies. The Outer Banks is considered to be the best surf-fishing venue in the world. The vast, open beaches between the Nags Head Pier and Jennette's Pier are easy to reach, with good access for angling. The Albemarle Sound and the Pamlico Sound provide the richest estuaries along the entire East Coast of the United States. The fishing villages of Rodanthe, Waves and Salvo, due south of Oregon Inlet, are the westernmost beaches along the entire barrier island chain. A little farther south, you will come upon the fishing village of Avon, where you will find the famous Avon Fishing Pier. The next stop along Highway 12 brings you to Cape Hatteras. Cape Hatteras is the undisputed surf-fishing capital of the world. The surrounding towns of Buxton, Frisco and Hatteras are geared toward fishing. Check out the Red Drum Tackle Shop to find out which fish are being caught. Our sport is the lifeblood of the area! Taking the ferry over Hatteras Inlet to Ocracoke Island will deliver you to yet another excellent surfcasting venue. Anywhere between Hatteras and

Ocracoke Inlets are prime fishing locations. My favorite venue for fishing on the island is up near Ramp #68. While on Ocracoke, make certain to visit Ride the Wind Surf Shop, where my college buddy Bob Chestnut will give you the local rundown. Portsmouth Island to Cape Lookout will afford you another fifty miles of pristine beaches. I have filled many coolers with puppy drum and speckled trout on Cedar Island on the Pamlico Sound. Look for Spanish inside the channels. If fishing from a boat, seek out the shallow grass beds for speckled trout. Tarpon show up in the sound, where fresh-cut bait is a favorite. Fishing for speckled trout in the marshes off the Neuse River is productive, especially near Swan Island. Deploying fresh-cut bait or crabs will ensure a plentiful bounty of fish. On the northern end of the islands, the villages of Corolla, Duck and Nags Head are splendid locations to catch a variety of pelagic species of the beach. Make certain to take in some of the local historical sights, such as the Wright Brothers Memorial at Kitty Hawk. This area is the billfish capital of the world. Keep in mind that parts of the Outer Banks are regulated as to when and where you can drive on the beach.

South Carolina

The Grand Strand

This is the famous coastal section that runs south from Little River down to just north of Georgetown. The Myrtle Beach region offers very good opportunities to catch fish in the surf. One of the best locations to fish at the coast is at the Cherry Grove Inlet, just north of Myrtle Beach. A favorite for local anglers is the area known as the rocks at Tubbs Inlet. Also at the northernmost part of the state is Little River, which is home to one of the largest commercial fishing fleets. Murrells Inlet and Huntington Beach State Park are excellent fishing venues nearly all year round for puppy drum and croaker.

Georgetown Area

The surf between Litchfield and DeBordieu Island provides plentiful opportunities to catch flounder, whiting and mackerel. The inlet is excellent for landing sheepshead and puppy drum. The Great Pee Dee

River pours into the backwaters of the bay and keeps things pretty stirred up. Fishing from the old Highway 17 bridge behind the hotels has always afforded us plenty of action in the summer months. Try bottom jigging with a red and white buck tail lead head around the piling of the bridge. The water is low in salinity and somewhat brackish, which can afford many species of fish. South of Winyah Bay is pretty remote until you get to the Bulls Bay area.

Charleston Area

Hands down, Charleston is the crown jewel of the South Carolina coast. Charleston is unique in that it is the convergence point of the Cooper and Ashley Rivers. As for surf fishing, the Isle of Palms is a popular destination for surfcasting. Wild Dunes is a very nice, secluded community that is fun to fish, if you know where. The best location at Wild Dunes is the transition zone between the salt marsh and the creeks that back up to the #2 golf course. Plenty of trout and redfish are caught in these backwaters in the spring and fall. Sullivan's Island and Mount Pleasant are great locations to catch a mixed bag of the indigenous species. Fishing at Breech Inlet, which separates the two islands, is very productive for flounder and croaker. Two of my favorite locations on the Ashley River side are the yacht basin at Wappoo Creek and at Hampton Park next to The Citadel. Make certain you spend plenty of time in Charleston and visit the Historical District and the markets. Be sure to treat yourself to some benne wafers while in the Historic District. Plan on taking the ferry over to Fort Sumter for some sightseeing adventure. No visit to Charleston is complete without visiting Boone Hall and Magnolia Plantations. On the Cooper River side of Charleston, Daniel Island and the Wando River are productive almost year round. Check in at Haddrell's Point Tackle and Supply in Mount Pleasant for "what's being caught in the Lowcountry." You will find good fishing at Patriots Point along the jetties and small seawalls. Cross James Island over to Folly Island on Highway 171 and you will find Folly Beach. Folly Beach is a very popular tourist destination for surf anglers. I have always had very good fortune sight casting to the schools of bluefish that run along Folly Beach.

Kiawah and Seabrook Islands

These backwaters provide some of the best flounder fishing along the South Carolina coast. Fishing the sound side of these islands will be more productive than fishing the open surf. The islands have a gradual slope that has been productive for croaker and spot. Farther south is Edisto Island and Edisto Beach. Bulls Bay and North Edisto Inlet are great for catching drum on cut bait. St. Helena and Hunting Island State Park is good but inconsistent for catching fish from the surf.

Beaufort, Bluffton and Port Royal

These are popular fishing spots behind miles of sand barrier islands that protect the salt marshes. The inlets that lead to the estuaries serve as a breeding ground for a multitude of pelagic species. I have heard many stories of good fishing across the water at Parris Island Marine Corps Base. The base is restricted, and thus, I have never had the good fortune of fishing its hallowed shores. My father was a Marine riflery coach on Parris Island during World War II, prior to shipping out to fight in the South Pacific. Semper Fidelis, Dad.

Hilton Head to Savannah

The best fishing in and around Hilton Head Island is over by Port Royal Plantation and Sea Pines. Everyone loves to fish the bay behind Shelter Cove for speckled trout and pompano. These bays and estuaries are protected by the barrier island and provide rich, essential nutrients for juvenile fish. Daufuskie Island has produced many large hauls of kingfish and blues during the fall migratory runs at the inlet. Fripp Island is not a very accessible venue for fishing. However, Fripp Island is home to my favorite author and our native son, Pat Conroy.

GEORGIA

Of all the locations on the Atlantic seaboard, Georgia offers the most rugged and undisturbed coastline. This is not at all a bad thing. Vacant beaches and limited commercial distractions will afford you an enjoyable day of seclusion. The state's untamed shoreline is approximately 210 miles long. Georgia experiences the most drastic tidal variations, up to a variance of seven feet. During a full moon, the tide is drastic and changes suddenly. A few of the state's nautical acres are still held by families dating back to the War Between the States. Reaching an accessible location in Georgia is made more difficult in that much of the shoreline and eleven of its thirteen barrier islands are private property. Others are owned and managed by state and local governmental agencies. The Georgia Department of Marine Fisheries publishes an annual guide with size and bag limits. At the time of this writing, red drum that measure over twenty-three inches must be released. Red drum of this size are in their prime for spawning, which helps the species prosper.

Tybee Island

This is my favorite place to fish in Georgia. I have had a great deal of success fishing at the lighthouse on the north end at the jetty. Wade out ten or so feet and cast just a foot or so shy of the rocks. Deploying a double-bottom rig baited with shrimp will afford you a cooler full of fish within a couple of hours. In addition to the excellent fishing on Tybee is the proximity to historical Savannah. Excellent accommodations and delightful restaurants make for a wonderful getaway to the coast.

Jekyll Island

The flats and sandbars along Georgia's southeastern coast afford you good red drum fishing. The Downing and Musgrove Causeways connect Brunswick to Jekyll Island. This area is highly productive from October to March for sheepshead and black drum. St. Simons Island produces some of the richest flounder fishing during the summer months on the north point. Use glass minnows or live shrimp to fill your cooler while enjoying the gorgeous scenery. The Savannah, Ogeechee and Altamaha Rivers and their inlets hold excellent weakfish and puppy drum in the late spring and early summer. Speckled trout is a hot species in St. Andrews Sound in the early spring and late fall. The specs are more readily caught when the water in the sound is clear and clean.

FLORIDA

Jacksonville to the Florida Keys is legendary for fishing. Fort Lauderdale to Miami Beach is primarily a boaters' haven of marinas filled with million-dollar sport-fishing yachts. Islamorada, "The Purple Island," was named by the Spanish for the native flower with purple vegetation. Islamorada is known as the offshore sport-fishing capital of the country. Fishing for small tarpon is very popular for inshore anglers wanting a good challenge. Pompano are the winter headliners on the Florida coast. Boynton Beach is an excellent close-in location that will not disappoint any fishermen. The Indian and St. Johns Rivers provide the best large drum fishing in the state. The Crystal River area is a wonderful inshore spot to catch pompano throughout the year. Fishing for red drum from Mosquito Lagoon to Fort Pierce is productive even on those cold days when the trout and pompano are not cooperating. Just south of Cape Canaveral toward Melbourne is very productive for mackerel, blues and croaker fishing with cut bait. Biscayne Bay is probably one of the top five spots on the eastern seaboard to catch tarpon. The majority of these fish are landed late in the afternoon, overnight into early morning.

A major advantage to fishing the Florida Coast is its proximity to the Gulf Stream. You can almost cast to the Gulf Stream from lower Miami Beach. The warm waters of the Gulf Stream flow right off the beach of Miami and quickly triangulate farther offshore onward to the west coast of the British Isles. To give you an idea, you can reach the Gulf Stream from Miami in less than five minutes by boat. By comparison, departing from Holden Beach, North Carolina, it takes over three hours traveling at twenty knots. The continental shelf is narrower along the coast of Florida than anywhere else on the eastern seaboard. These two variables help put Florida at the forefront of offshore sport fishing. The peninsula's subtropical climate, with high humidity and seasonally warm temperatures, affords anglers year-round fishing conditions. Pompano, Spanish mackerel and blues are ever-present in the Sunshine State.

The Florida Panhandle is excellent for fishing from inshore on a flats boat. From Key West to Pensacola and everywhere in between—Tampa Bay, Cedar Key, Boca Grand, Sarasota, St. Petersburg, Marco Island, Port Charlotte—much of the coastal sections of the Florida Gulf Coast are developed and are reasonably accessible to anglers. The salt marshes that run north to south from Port St. Joe are very productive fishing grounds. The mangroves are under federal protection and have been since the

1970s. The tidal marshes around these mangroves are excellent for trout and red drum. The state of Florida highly regulates which fish can be kept and the slot limits. Florida does require a saltwater fishing license.

THE GULF COAST

Alabama

Given that Alabama has a limited amount of shoreline, the majority of anglers head offshore in fancy sport-fishing boats. Mobile Bay, Pinto Pass, the Mobile River and Gulf Shores are about the only productive inshore locations. The remains of the old Dauphin Island Bridge and the surrounding oyster beds is by far the best shore fishing that consistently produces plenty of fish season after season.

Mississippi

The Pascagoula River inlet and Delacroix are excellent venues for inshore saltwater game fish. Excellent catches of trout are normal in these waters. However, Mississippi is best known for producing trophy freshwater fish, such as largemouth bass and catfish.

Louisiana

The multitude of estuaries and backwater bays and bayous creates some of the most productive inshore fishing along the entire Gulf Coast region. Areas such as Baptiste Collette Bayou, the Dixie Bar and Venice are known more for quantity of fish than the size of saltwater game fish.

Texas

The Badlands, Galveston Bay, East Matagorda Bay, Port Aransas, Lower Laguna Madre, the Mexican border at Brownsville—each of these venues produces some of the best fishing in the Gulf. Texas hosts more redfish tournaments than any other state in the union.

The Gulf Coast dead zone occurs each year during the spring runoff when the Mississippi River carries oxygen-depleted water from urban and farm areas into the Gulf of Mexico. Nutrient-laden fresh water from the Mississippi remains at the surface of Gulf coastal waters. These nutrients promote growth of algae at the surface, which feeds plankton and fish. Dead algae and fish waste sink to the seafloor and are decomposed by bacteria. The bacteria consumes oxygen, which has caused widespread fish kills over the past three decades.

Mexico

The Yucatan Peninsula is seemingly better suited for anglers in sport-fishing boats. The most successful surf fishing is north of Cabo San Lucas, which provides bountiful fishing almost year round.

NOTE: The infamous BP oil spill of 2010 has for the most part been mitigated. The impact on fish and wildlife was far less dramatic than originally thought. The seafood being harvested from the Gulf Coast is excellent. I have fished the region since the BP disaster and am pleased to report the fishing conditions are very good.

NOTABLE FISHING VENUES AT A DISTANCE

The Amazon Delta of Central Peru

Fishing for peacock bass in Peru on the Amazon River was an unforgettable experience. The fish species weigh in at an impressive average of twelve pounds and is nearly two feet in length. Landing the peacock requires . patience, stamina and keeping your limbs clear of water hazards. Our guide kept a shotgun at his side to fend off any crocodiles or large anacondas. We fished for this species south of Cuzco, Peru, after flying into the Amazon Delta on a floatplane. My guide was a much better fisherman than a pilot. Apparently, earning a pilot's license is not very demanding or regulated in South America. Only after our trip did we question how he honed his skills of flying very low through the trees in the Amazon rain forest. We were able to ascertain that he was a distribution pilot for one of the local "pharmaceutical" manufacturers. Our guide was able to redeem himself by preparing an excellent dinner of our sautéed bass with plantains. I highly recommend fishing for peacock bass in the Amazon and taking the train through the Andes Mountains to Machu Picchu.

The Great Barrier Reef in Australia

The Great Barrier Reef off the eastern coast of Queensland, Australia, was spectacular. We departed on our quest from the port at Cairns in a small, antiquated boat that was scarcely seaworthy to fish the reef. The seas were rough, but the fishing was spectacular. I caught over fifteen species of native fish, including a five-foot-long great white shark. We safely released everything that we caught back into the Coral Sea.

The Nile River in Egypt

I had an exhilirating time while battling Nile perch in the River Nile in lower Egypt some two hundred kilometers south of Cairo. My Egyptian guide was quick to point out how coveted the species is for table fare at the finest restaurants in North Africa. We did sample the species that night for dinner, prepared in the traditional Egyptian method of poaching. The species tastes much like rainbow trout caught in the Appalachian Mountains.

Chapter 12

Fishing from Piers, Bridges and Structures

Over the past century and a half, fishing piers have served as the central focus of many beach towns. As land values skyrocketed, fishing piers have become fewer in number. The piers attract tourism in the spring, summer and fall, drawing the same anglers year after year. But increasing land values, taxes and insurance premiums threaten the existence of the remaining fishing piers. Most fishing piers charge a daily fee of less than ten dollars for anglers to fish. Some piers charge a usage price or fee per rod. It is in the best interest of everyone to help keep and support the local piers. These piers represent a part of our heritage and should be preserved for future generations to enjoy. Pulling in fish "over the rail" is very satisfying.

Fishing from bridges allows the angler access to deep, moving water while providing a dry yet stable platform from which to operate. Many vehicular bridges prohibit fishing. I have been ushered off numerous elevated roadways over the years. Be mindful of passing traffic as you handle your gear, tackle and especially your rods. Do not step onto the roadway and into the path of any traffic. Remember, you are working with very little space with little room for error. Do not allow or take any children onto active bridges where speeding cars are only inches away. Bridges are very productive man-made habitats for fishing. Bridges offer everything that a game fish could want. Most every coastal bridge crosses deep water where fish feel safe and somewhat protected. The pilings help provide a constant disruption in the water as the current moves in and out. This is an excellent place for fish to ambush bait. Not only do the pilings expose baitfish, but they are also encrusted with barnacles, which host crabs and mussels. Baiting your rig with finger mullet worked down flow from the pilings is very productive. Be mindful not to allow your rig to be washed and hung up in the underwater structure. Try to visualize the submerged barnacle-covered pilings and keep your rig and line clear to avoid your line being cut. Be aware that when your rig comes free of the water, it will have a tendency to swing under the bridge and become wrapped up in the understructure. As the terminal tackle clears the water, there is a sudden release of resistance, which can tangle your terminal tackle under the bridge's pilings. Slow your retrieve just prior to your rig clearing the water.

PIER FISHING

From Virginia to Florida, there are nearly sixty fishing piers, give or take what the current Atlantic hurricane season delivers the southeastern Atlantic coastline. The majority are open to the public, while a few are privately owned. Most of our piers have seen their share of battle damage. Many of the piers from yesteryear have disappeared due to hurricanes or new development. Pier fishing is an extension of surf fishing. There are a lot of positive attributes to standing on a nice solid wooden pier. Much less gear is required when fishing from the pier. Pretty much, you park your car right in front, carry your rod up the ramp to the tackle shop, purchase your bait and cold soda and off you go to pull fish over the rail. Walk a hundred feet or so, pick a bench, bait up and cast. If you elect to carry a cooler and other gear with you, that is okay too. Carrying yourself and gear down the pier is so much easier than dragging all your gear through the soft sand all the way down the beach. There has been occasion when I have not had enough time to dedicate to a full day of surf fishing. Taking a single rod to the pier can get you wet in a matter of minutes, especially if you are fishing with artificial bait or lures. Not having to deal with cutting and hooking bait is another plus, if you desire. More often than not, pier fishermen deploy cut bait like shrimp or bloodworm with a double hook bottom rig. Seasoned pier fishing veterans pursue fishing two hours prior to an incoming high tide, especially when it occurs in the morning around the break of dawn. Fishing on overcast days is usually more productive than a bright, sunny day.

A few rules of the pier include not to cross over others' lines and to avoid hooking people behind you. Fishing off the pier requires that you pay close attention to everyone in your vicinity. Many piers allow visitors to roam the planks. This poses a constant problem of having non-fishermen in your presence. They tend to not look where they are walking and talking. Keep your cast to a short and simple overhead cast. This will give you maximum control of your rig. Remember, you are responsible for your gear and anyone who may be on the receiving end of an errant cast. Swinging three-plus ounces of lead festooned with hooks can be lethal. Be careful when reeling in your rig that you do not get hung up on the wooden structural crossbeams. Time your retrieval to avoid becoming snagged on the upswing as you bring up your rig. When fishing from the pier, your rig will suddenly come out of the water and can get hung up under the pier. If you hook a large fish, you may require use of the pier's retrieval net. This net is lowered into the water with the help of another person to haul up a heavy fish. Trying to lift a big fish out of the water without a net can be costly. Straightened hooks or broken line will often be the unfortunate result. Remember, do not bring your lure or rig out of the water too fast. The best book about fishing piers is by my friend and fellow author Al Baird, *North Carolina Coastal Fishing Piers*, published by The History Press.

ESCALADES AND EXCURSIONS

Many hard-core surf anglers drive expensive, four-wheel-drive sport utility vehicles to fish on the beach. These expensive behemoths are usually equipped with a complete arsenal of components used to surf fish, such as a cooler and a surf rod rack. Several rules of the road for driving on the beach:

- Use only four-wheel-drive vehicles. Do not attempt to drive in the sand with a two-wheel-drive auto.
- Always deflate your tires for maximum traction in the soft sand.
- The average extrication fee to pull you off the beach is $300 (assuming that the tow truck gets to you before the incoming tide does).
- Always monitor the tides to ensure that you do not get cut off from the access road.
- Drive only where permitted.
- Do not disturb the ecology, plants, turtles or other species.
- At night, dim your lights when driving to and from the beach. It is not good to scare our little fish friends.
- Pedestrians always have the right of way. Be very careful of families and children!

- Invest in one of those fancy trailer mount rod/cooler holders. They are cool and very practical.
- Make certain that you wash your vehicle and the undercarriage after each trip.

Fortunately or unfortunately, depending on your environmental perspective, vehicular access to beaches is becoming increasingly scarce over time. Privatization and environmental pressures have greatly reduced driving access to the ocean's edge. Concerns over the habitat of indigenous species of turtles and waterfowl have prompted stricter regulation. Do not look for increased access anytime soon. Several state courts are hearing arguments over the privilege, but do not expect litigation to favor the 4 X 4 enthusiast. With the increased awareness agenda of "going green," environmentalists are having their way in the legislature in regard to the issue. Many of my favorite fishing grounds are becoming off-limits to vehicular traffic. Many jurisdictions require that you obtain a permit to drive on the beach.

Chapter 13

Surf, Sand, Beach
and Weather Conditions

Locating fish requires being able to detect subtle contours and characteristics in the surf that attract and hold fish. Elements such as the weather and beach formations factor into locating fish. When the barometer is changing, the upper atmosphere is the first to change. Jet airplanes produce a contrail from their turbine engines. Observing these vapor trails can give you a good indication of atmospheric conditions. When you see the sky full of many long and somewhat unbroken exhaust contrails, the air is moist and saturated. Many times, you will observe an aircraft in the sky with little or no contrail. This indicates that the air mass is dry. What is happening is that the moisture coming off the engines forms a frozen fog or ice crystal of sorts. When the air is moist, the vapor maintains its form and produces this icy fog that catches the sunlight and is visible to the human eye.

The greatest difference between ebb and high tide occurs during the new and full moons of each month. Fishing at night is traditionally more productive for larger fish. Do not be apprehensive about fishing in the dark. Go prepared and well equipped. Fishing under a moonlit sky makes for optimum conditions. Less water movement occurs during the moon's first and third quarters. Rising and receding tides are premium fishing periods.

Foul weather offshore will encourage feeding. The approach of storm fronts usually triggers a brief feeding frenzy. Fish react to atmospheric changes in the barometer. Game fish will feed very aggressively before and often during a storm. Fish seem to stock up ahead of time, as they do not know what changes lie ahead as far as their food supply is concerned. After

●	New Moon	○		Full Moon	
◐	Waxing crescent	◑		Waning gibbous	
◑	First quarter		◑	Last quarter	
○	Waxing gibbous	◐		Waning crescent	

a storm front has passed, the fish feed very aggressively. However, the water is usually dirty and stirred up pretty well, causing havoc with your rigs. Even moderate rainfall changes the salinity content in the water. Turbulence is formed when water rushes over a structure, creating rips and upwellings. The sandbar displaces and compresses the water, which increases its flow speed. This results in breaking water, creating standing waves and rip current, which stirs up food and baitfish within the water column.

You can calculate your distance from an approaching storm by counting the seconds from seeing the lightning to hearing the thunder. Lightning is very hot and super heats the air very quickly. The air expands violently and then quickly contracts. The rapid explosion of the air creates sound waves that we hear as thunder. When lightning strikes, we see it instantaneously due to the fact that it travels at the speed of light, which is 186 thousand miles per second. The sound waves or thunder travels much slower, at 1,000 feet per second. Thus, we see the lightning before we hear the thunder. Since there are 5,280 feet in a mile, thunder will travel approximately 1 mile for every five seconds. If you count to five before you hear thunder, the lightning strike is about one mile away; counting to ten puts the lightning at two miles away. If the sky is illuminating in the distance but we fail to receive the audible report of thunder, the storm is several miles away. This is referred to as heat lightning.

Take advantage of cold or rainy weather and go through and clean your gear and straighten out your tackle box. Pre-arrange your rigs in Ziploc baggies to keep them organized and tangle-free. Remember, you want to get your line into the water as quickly as possible.

The wind is always a variable to contend with at the coast. We must cope with the wind's direction and intensity. There have been occasions when the wind is too strong to cast my rig. One of the biggest challenges is when the wind catches your deployed line like a sail and pushes your rig back onto the beach. You can try a heavier sinker, but using too much lead will deplete your feel of a strike. Often, this leads to your bait being stolen by carnivore crabs or pesky pinfish.

Water temperature plays an important role in fishing. Every angler should be in tune with even the subtlest of variance. Game fish are no different from other species when it comes to cold or hot. Fish move within the water column to maintain a temperature that is to their liking. Water temperature will dictate where the fish gather and where they feed at various times of the year. Each and every species of fish has a temperature range that it prefers. When water temperatures rise above the fifty-degree mark, the fish will begin to actively feed. The month of October will usher in cooler weather and bring the fish back in toward shore. Traditionally, the middle of October through early December provides the best fishing for those of us along the southeastern coast.

During the colder months, most species of fish have a reduced appetite. Locating the fish when they are ready to consume is the challenge. Fish are coldblooded organisms that adapt to the temperature of their environment. The temperature in the water column greatly contributes to whether fish are foraging for a meal. During the winter months especially, the majority of heat from the sun is absorbed on the water surface. Depending on the flow of the current, the temperature within the water column will fluctuate at different depths. These temperature breaks are known as thermoclines, which change frequently.

The southeastern coast is very prone to visits from hurricanes and other very strong storms. Usually, the fishing is quite good on the days leading up to the arrival of a storm. However, for up to a week after the storm clouds have cleared, the beach has extensive erosion problems and the surf is loaded with seaweed. If you are able to get a line in the water and avoid the seaweed, the fishing is magnificent the day after the storm clears out. Trying to fish the surf with an abundance of seaweed washing in is next to impossible. Large blobs of seaweed will wash over your rig. Your rod will bend, even shake a little. To top it all off, the current will move your rig around to the point that you are certain that you have a trophy fish on the end of your line. This is not at all the case. If you are able to retrieve your rig, everything will be wrapped up in seaweed. Trying to free your rig of this mess after an hour will send you packing it to the creeks, backwaters or the sound.

TROPICAL WEATHER TERMINOLOGY

TROPICAL DEPRESSION: Condensed thunderstorms within a cyclonic rotation. Winds up to thirty-eight miles per hour.

TROPICAL STORM: Severe thunderstorms within a cyclonic circulation. Wind speeds between thirty-nine and seventy-five miles per hour.

HURRICANE: Closed cyclonic storm with sustained winds of seventy-four miles per hour or greater.

HURRICANE WATCH: Issued for coastal regions where landfall is threatened within forty-eight hours.

HURRICANE WARNING: Issued when a hurricane is expected to make landfall within thirty-six hours.

The official hurricane season begins June 1 and ends November 30. The tropical storms and hurricanes we experience along the southern Atlantic coastline usually originate off the coast of West Africa. Hurricanes produce deadly storm surges, life-threatening winds and other unforeseen dangers to life and property. Hurricanes are categorized between 1 and 5, using the Saffir-Simpson Hurricane Scale based on barometric pressure and wind speed. Stay alert and informed of potential storms and follow evacuation orders when issued by local emergency management authorities.

Chapter 14

Bait Shops, Boat Docks and Surfer Dudes

Maybe it's just me, but I think not—local bait and tackle shops up and down the southeastern coast vary on the level of support or advice they will offer you. I would say that nearly two-thirds of these local bait and tackle shops cater to their local clientele. Many, if not all, of the merchants at these bait and tackle shops can spot an out-of-towner when he walks in the door. Do not expect the gentleman behind the counter to confide in you the best venue as to where the fish are being caught. He will gladly sell you bait and tackle, usually at fair market value. I have been witness to many a blank stare when a shopkeeper is asked where the fish are hitting and what they are being caught with. It has been suggested that some bait shops will insist that the bait the fish are hitting is what they have the most of in the cooler. At the risk of hindering the sale of this book, I will refrain from mentioning which shops condone this style of customer service. Rest assured that any store carrying this book is the exception and can be trusted as a merchant of high ethical, moral and business standards. Feel free to spend plenty of cash on whatever these fine people suggest. If you do not see this book on the shelf, leave until you find a good and proper store that does carry my title.

CROWDED BEACHES AND SURFER DUDES

Not even the salty old-timers have been able to share or confirm why fishermen and surfers do not get along. Let's see—could it be that we are both seeking sovereign control over the same aquatic real estate? This has to be where the hostilities originate. When I was a kid, the surfers would come in close to the fishing pier and tempers would flare. I cannot confirm or deny that some anglers were casting at these moving targets. This has the same appeal as a golfer on the driving range taking aim at the guy driving the ball cart. Whatever the situation, anglers need to coexist with those around us. Besides, we are heavily armed with big rods, weights and those nasty hooks. Many non-anglers can become very intimidated when the lead is flying.

CAPTAIN'S QUARTERS

Count on seeing "No Fishing" or "Boat Owners Only" signs posted at almost every marina. Fishing in and around marinas and yacht basins makes every sailor and boat owner nervous. Boat slips are sort of like private property. The owners really do not want uninvited guests yielding hooks and weights around their expensive vessels. This activity is as well received as letting kids race shopping carts at a Porsche dealership. Boat owners expect a certain degree of privacy and do not welcome any disturbance while sipping their prosecco on the aft deck. No one wants a broken window or a hook buried in a mooring line. However, many docks along the backwaters are void of boats and are good fishing locations, assuming you can secure permission.

Chapter 15

Hurricanes and Hush Puppies

PLEASE PASS THE HUSH PUPPIES

The entire southern United States is special in a multitude of ways. The original title for this book was to refer to fishing the coast of the Carolinas. After considerable thought, I decided it best to be more inclusive and cover the area from Virginia to Florida. Well, after yet more consideration, I thought it best to include the Gulf Coast as well. With this disclosure, I confess my affinity to being partial to North and South Carolina. Lake Wylie is the freshwater lake in the Upstate of South Carolina where I grew up fishing and honing my angling skills. That being said, I have taken the liberty of sharing some cultural, historical and anecdotal perspective of the two Carolinas. Follow along and become enlightened as to what has shaped us into who we are today. It is altogether possible that if you take a look at the fabric of what defines our region, you may adopt some of our unique and proper culture. Not only does our venue produce the finest in saltwater fishing but also a very unique style of seafood preparation. Down here in the South, we have perfected and prefer our seafood prepared á la Calabash style. What is Calabash? Calabash is a small fishing village in North Carolina just a smidgeon above the state line with South Carolina. This is the place where breaded, deep-fried seafood got its start. Schedule a trip to the Grand Strand for the best seafood in the South. Afterward, head over to the OD Pavilion to shag to some of our classic beach music.

Back in the glorious period of the antebellum South, much of the southern coastal region was home to expansive and stately plantations. Our plantations were for the most part the primary source of the southern economy. The majority of these estates were producing staples such as cotton, rice, indigo or wheat. Plantation houses of the period were under the ever-present and looming threat of fire. The majority of plantation fires were accidentally started in the kitchen or were set courtesy of General William Tecumseh Sherman during the War Between the States. We loyal southerners begrudgingly afford General Sherman contributory liability as to much of our destruction as he marched to the sea.

Other plantation houses were built with the kitchen being an outbuilding, constructed separately from the main house to reduce the likelihood of fire. Problem solved? No, not exactly. Plantations were dependent on slave labor. Not only did the servants work the fields, but they also served as domestics. The servants would cook and bring the food up from the kitchen to the main house to serve the family meals. Many of these wealthy plantation owners were avid hunters who had packs of hunting dogs. The dogs would smell the food being prepared and gather outside the kitchen in anticipation of handouts. The servants would skillet fry cornbread scraps in lard. Come dinnertime, when the meals were being walked up to the big house, the servants would satisfy the aggressive dogs' appetites with these treats while saying, "Hush, puppy." This delicacy is now the standard side dish served with our delicious fried fish, shrimp, oysters and, of course, barbecue.

Hurricanes and nor'easters have laid waste to most of the coast at one time or another. Many of our piers, beaches and homes have seen their share of battle damage over the years. Tropical storms and hurricanes are a way of life if you reside at the ocean. One such storm prevented a Spanish assault on Charles Towne, South Carolina, in 1686 by destroying the ship's galleys and killing the fleet's commodore. Memorable storms that have made landfall along the southeastern United States coast include:

- The Galveston Hurricane of 1900 claimed nearly ten thousand souls when it decimated Galveston Island, Texas, at the turn of the century.
- Hurricane Hazel made landfall at Little River, South Carolina, in October 1954.
- Hurricane Camille is considered to be the worst storm to hit the mainland of the United States. Camille devastated the Mississippi

Gulf Coast on August 18, 1969, with winds in excess of two hundred miles per hour.

- Hurricane David made landfall in Georgia, just south of Savannah, in 1979.
- Hurricane Hugo made landfall in 1989 near Sullivan's Island and the Isle of Palms before moving inward through Charlotte with tropical storm force winds. Hugo was the costliest storm up to that time, with damages in excess of $7 billion.
- Hurricane Andrew was one of Florida's costliest cyclones in history when it made landfall at Homestead, Florida, in 1992.
- Tropical Storm Alberto came inland from the Florida Panhandle on July 4, 1994, producing catastrophic flooding, which led to thirty deaths. Florida has paid the deadliest price in regard to hurricane fatalities.
- The Labor Day Hurricane of 1935 and the Okeechobee Hurricane of 1928 killed thousands when the storms swept their victims into the lake when the back side of the eye wall passed.
- Hurricanes Dennis and Floyd killed more than thirty-five people in North Carolina, mostly from flooding, in 1995.
- Hurricane Fran moved inland in 1996, bringing destruction to the Research Triangle Park in North Carolina.
- Hurricane Katrina formed over the Bahamas in late August 2005. After crossing over the Florida peninsula, Katrina laid waste to New Orleans and its neighboring parishes with devastating floods. The failure of the levee systems in New Orleans is considered to be the worst civil engineering disaster in U.S. history. Over 1,800 people perished when local residents failed to evacuate as instructed. Hurricane Katrina was the most costly hurricane in U.S. history, with damages exceeding $100 billion.

Chapter 16

Table Fare Preparation, Field Dressing and Cleaning

Somehow we possess an inherent trait that gives us satisfaction from consuming the bounty harvested with our own hands. Our palates have become more refined than in generations past. We are no longer appeased with bland, uncomplicated tastes of years gone by. In order to maximize the freshest quality of your catch, it must be properly prepared in the field upon capture. The less your fish is exposed to air, the better the flavor. A smart angler will have an idea in advance of how he intends to prepare and consume his fish. The method in which you field dress and clean your quarry is dictated by your plan of culinary preparation. If you plan on cooking your fish the very same day that they are caught, keep them fresh and slime-free by doing the following: Fill your bounty cooler with ice and a few gallons of seawater. This mixture will become very slushy and remain cold, which will keep your fish fresh. This solution will ensure that your fish will be kept prime until you are ready to dress them for cooking.

A fish that you plan to eat must be kept fresh. The best way to ensure that your fish remains fresh is to keep it alive until it is ready to be cleaned. Do not let your fish remain in cold, melted ice water. If you plan to clean all your fish at one time, keep your cooler's drain plug open and keep adding plenty of fresh ice on your fish throughout the day. I have witnessed some old-timers bury their freshly caught fish in the sand in hopes of keeping it cool until they are ready to leave the beach. I have also witnessed a beagle digging up a fully intact Spanish mackerel that was apparently buried and misplaced by its captor.

When purchased from a store, whole fish should always have bright red blood present. If the blood is slimy and brownish in color, the fish is not fresh and should not be consumed. Look at the gills; again, a bright red color is desirable. The eyes should be clear and open, not cloudy and dull. The same is true for shellfish such as shrimp and crab. Never consume clams or mussels that do not separate after cooking. If you have any concerns about the smell or appearance of raw seafood, do not consume it.

The key to proper freezing of your fish is to reduce air exposure to the flesh when packaging for freezing. After proper cleaning, place your fish in a quality freezer bag and immerse in water to force the air out. Freezing your fish quickly will help maintain its flavor. Place each package of fish directly on the freezing surface. Another popular method for preserving fish is to freeze them completely submerged in water.

Species such as croaker, spot and kingfish are best scaled, headed and gutted. These species are best prepared in this method due to having many bones. Trying to cut a proper fillet from these species usually will result in wasted fish. Larger species of fish are prepared by filleting. The purpose of filleting is to provide pieces of fish without bones. Regardless of how you prepare your fish, proper and complete removal of scales is paramount. It is very important that fish scales remain moist for proper removal. Move your scaling implement from tail to head. Proper removal of the fish head is to cut with ample pressure to cut through the backbone. The initial cut should be behind the head and the pectoral fins. Cut on both sides of your fish, behind the gills, at a forty-five-degree angle to get the maximum yield of meat. Cut the entire length of the belly, from anal vent to the head. Remove all intestines and organs from the body cavity. Rinse with water to remove any residual matter. Be careful when removing the fins from your fish to avoid getting stuck. Flounder and pompano are best filleted. When filleting, it is not necessary to head and gut the fish. Proficiency with a sharp, flexible fillet knife is an essential requirement to becoming a good angler. Several species of fish must be bled and iced immediately after being caught to ensure flavor and freshness. For bluefish and sharks, make a fairly deep incision about one inch above the caudal fin.

The following are the most popular techniques to field dress fish:

SCALING: The process of removing the scales from the skin of a fish. Scale fish on a flat surface using one hand to hold it by the head. Rake the scales from the tail toward the head with a scaling device. Flip your quarry over and repeat the process. All recipes call for removal of fish scales if the meat is not filleted.

GUTTING: This process involves removing the fish's head. This is done using a sharp knife and cutting between the gills and the pectoral fins. Next, fully cleanse the fish's internal cavity. This is completed by inserting the knife into the fish's anal vent and slicing forward toward the head. Insert your finger and completely remove all internal organs. Deposit the fish's remains back into the ocean. Consider this recycling and completing the circle of life.

FILLETING: The process in which you skillfully cut away the skin to expose the meat that is to be consumed. The process involves using a flexible fillet knife to cut very close to the bone in order to yield the greatest amount of meat. Filleting involves removing the meat of the fish without the bones. Most large species that are kept as table fare are filleted. A properly filleted fish has its skin and all of its bones removed prior to cooking. Scaling is not necessary, as the skin is being removed. To fillet fish, lay it on its side on a flat, stable surface. Cut the fish behind its gills and pectoral fin down to, but not through, the backbone. Without removing your knife, rotate the blade and cut above the ribs toward the tail. Use the fish's backbone to navigate your progress. Repeat the process on the other side. Finally, insert your knife blade close to the rib bones and carefully slice the entire rib section away from each fillet. Next, with the skin side down, insert your knife blade approximately a quarter inch away from the tail. Holding the tail firmly with your free hand, place your knife blade between the meat and the skin. The sharp edge of your blade should be at a slight angle delicately touching the skin. Using very little pressure, with a slow sawing motion, cut against, not through, the skin. You should end up with a perfectly dissected fillet. Rinse each fillet in fresh, cold water and pat dry with a paper towel. Seal your fresh fillets immediately in an airtight baggie and keep them cold until ready to cook. Minimize the amount of air that comes into contact with the meat to retain freshness.

STEAKING: A process in which large fish such as sharks or king mackerel are prepared into steaks. First things first, clean, scale and cut. High-end restaurants chill the fish in the freezer prior to cutting, as this affords easier cutting. Work your way from the tail to the head, cutting one- to two-inch thick steaks. After completion of cutting, trim away any excess fat or bones that are visible. Do not attempt to remove the backbone. Rinse, pat dry and store in airtight baggies until ready to grill. Steaking is the simplest method of dressing your catch. The proper manner to prepare fish in the style is to remove all the internal organs by gutting your fish. Sharks are one of the most popular species prepared in this fashion.

SKINNING: The method in which the fish's epidermal layer or skin is separated from the meat. Skinning is usually part of the filleting process if you intend to prepare your fillets as chunks. Several species of fish are best prepared by removing the skin. Certain fish need the skin removed for palatable reasons. Bluefish are a prime candidate for skinning. This process can also be applied when the fish is being prepared for bone-in cooking.

CHUNKING: The process in which the meat of a fish is cut into cubes for stews, soups and chowders. Fish that are prepared using this method must have all bones for cooking. Most recipes call for fish to be cut into half-inch cubes for consistent results when preparing your culinary delight.

Chapter 17

Litigation and Libations

M any of our coastal communities are under legal jurisdictions that strictly regulate what you can and cannot have or do on the beach. Fireworks, alcohol and campfires are among the most objectionable offenses. Some locales disallow surf fishing on densely populated beaches between 9:00 a.m. and 5:00 p.m. to avoid beach-goers. Be aware of any local ordinances that may pertain to your group's planned activities. Pleading ignorance is not a valid defense to local magistrates and law enforcement. Most of these violations and infractions are misdemeanors. Here is a sample of the most common transgressions that pertain to all beach-goers.

POSSESSION/CONSUMPTION OF ALCOHOL: Many local municipalities strictly regulate alcohol consumption on the beach. Most forbid the use of glass bottles, for obvious reasons. I have witnessed many missteps by anglers who have partaken heavily in the libations. Many expensive fishing rods and reels have gone under water due to impairment.

WADING/SWIMMING: For the most part, swimming is prohibited in and around jetties and dangerous inlets where the water current can overtake a swimmer. Be mindful of submerged structures when swimming unfamiliar waters. Local officials can and do issue citations for swimming in unauthorized areas.

LITTERING: Many municipalities issue big fines for littering or leaving cigarette butts in the sand. This should be a moot point for anyone who enjoys our natural resources. While visiting the beach, be proactive and pick up any litter that others may have disregarded and dispose of it accordingly.

PARKING ENFORCEMENT: This is a big one! Parking in and around beach access points is strictly regulated. Many cars are ticketed or towed for parking in the wrong spot. Issuing parking tickets is big money for local municipalities.

RESTRICTED DRIVING—DUNES: There are fewer and fewer locations along the coast that allow driving on the beach. Resist driving on the beach if at all possible. Crossing over sand dunes is forbidden. Make certain that you stay off all the dunes. They protect the beach from storm damage and beach erosion and are a natural refuge for oceanic wildlife.

DRIVING PERMITS: Access to drive on most beaches now requires that you obtain a beach access permit. These permits must be purchased in the local municipality where you intend to fish.

TRESPASSING: Public beach easements for pedestrian access are well marked. Homeowners of expensive beachfront property do expect a certain degree of privacy. Be cognizant of posted signage. Crossing over sand dunes is strongly discouraged and can destroy vegetation such as sea oats.

FISHING LICENSES: Each state has laws that govern required fishing licenses. Make certain that everyone in your party has been issued the proper licenses and permits. Wildlife officers will not hesitate to issue you a ticket if you do not possess a fishing license.

FIREWORKS: Yes, many states sell them, but you can't use them. Besides, fireworks scare the fish.

WATERCRAFT VIOLATIONS: Launching watercraft from the beach is regulated as to when and where. Most every beach has boat ramps for launching boats. Follow the posted regulations. Law enforcement tends to frequent boat landings. Make certain that younger passengers are wearing USCG-approved flotation devices.

CREEL AND BAG LIMITS: Know exactly what size and number of fish you are allowed to keep. Be keenly aware that in coastal waters, it is unlawful to possess any fish without the head and tail attached if that species is subject to size and creel limits. This includes red drum, sea bass and flounder, just to name a few. Wildlife enforcement officers have been known to seize rods, reels and other treasure of those in violation. Do not keep any illegal fish! These regulations are in place to ensure that future generations can enjoy the sport.

Each state has its own regulations as to which fish you can catch and keep. They may relate to the fishing season and the length of the fish, as well as the number of fish (bag limit) that you are allowed to keep each day. These regulations are designed to maintain the various species and improve their populations. Know before you go. Log onto your state's wildlife or natural resource department's webpage for current regulations and advisories. Many states offer fishing citation awards for landing certain species. Your fish must meet minimum size or weight standards in order to receive your certificate. Official wildlife weigh stations are located up and down the entire southeastern coastline at bait and tackle shops or piers.

Chapter 18

Preservation, Prevention and Coastal Conservation

R ecreational anglers must take some of the responsibility of conservation of our aquatic environment. From a local position, each of us can contribute to the cause by keeping our beaches clean and free of debris and trash. I set an example for my children by picking up any trash I see on the beach, not just ours but what others have left behind as well. Make certain that you properly discard all used fishing line and hooks. These two items are not only waste but can also be dangerous to other people and wildlife. *Leave only your footprints*.

CONSERVATION

Successful coastal conservation will help ensure recovering stocks of all species. The potential impact of global warming could lead to melting glaciers and ice caps and rising sea levels. We must manage inland agricultural farmland to control runoff of pesticides and fertilizers and make sure they don't end up in our oceans. We must look beyond our local fishing grounds to ensure proper resource management. The issues affecting our coastal fishing grounds are being impacted from hundreds of miles away. Sport fishing provides bounties of enjoyment, satisfaction and occasionally a gourmet meal for millions of anglers. The sport fishing industry supports thousands of jobs throughout the country. Our industry has the support of good resource management through licenses and other voluntary standards.

Obtaining the proper coastal recreational fishing license(s) helps generate millions of dollars in revenue for managing our saltwater resources. Please participate in these efforts to help support our conservational initiatives. It is in the best interest to want to help preserve our pelagic species and help ensure that future generations will be able to enjoy the sport. Support environmental groups such as the Coastal Conservation Association.

BEACH SAFETY

Common aquatic mishaps include:

- Cutting one's hand with thy knife
- Laceration of the feet on shells and such
- The embedding of a fishhook into one's hand
- Sharing some of your skin with a jellyfish
- Slicing open a finger with fishing line
- Sunburn and windburn
- Stay off the beach during electrical storms
- Graphite fishing rods are very conductive and thus make for excellent lightning rods

Injuries from Sharks and Fish

If you are reading this fine book, chances are that you are a surfcasting aficionado. With that being said, it is understood that we put ourselves in the water at the ocean's edge to be at one with God's creatures. Precautionary advice goes against pretty much everything we do as anglers. Let's see—we are tossing freshly cut meat into the sea to attract fish. Newsflash—sharks also have a hankering for these tasty morsels that we present for consumption. Truth be told, you are more likely to be bitten by the likes of a bluefish than a shark. If you are experiencing the misfortune of an encounter with Jaws, here is what you do: use your fishing rod butt to stab at the nose or eyes and then retreat posthaste from the water. Here are the most common activities that attract sharks:

- Being in the water around dusk (the best time to fish)
- Displaying bright and shiny reflective objects (such as fishing lures)

- Movement in the water (like wading knee deep while fishing)
- The presence or scent of fresh meat in the water (like cut bait)

If you are bitten, you will have to deal with one or more of the following wounds:

- Puncture: Each tooth will leave a hole in your skin
- Laceration: Sharp teeth can easily rip and tear flesh
- Avulsion: Bad news—this is when a chunk of flesh is removed
- Fracture: Bad news again—strong jaw pressure can break bones

How to Escape a Rip Current

Rip currents are the most dangerous hazard to anyone in the surf. If you feel yourself being pulled away from the beach by these strong currents, don't panic and do not try to swim toward the beach. Swimming toward the beach is much like trying to swim upstream in a river. Instead, swim parallel to the beach to escape the strong current. When you feel that you are free from the current, turn and swim back to the beach. If you are unable to make it back to the beach, calmly stop swimming, face the beach, wave your hands and shout to attract attention to yourself.

Jellyfish and Stingray Treatment

Swimmers should allow jellyfish a wide berth to avoid contact with their long-reaching tentacles. The jellyfish species is evolutionarily programmed to respond and adapt to changes in their surroundings. The scorching hot days of late summer will usher in the arrival of the species. The sting from a jellyfish comes from the protruding tentacles that trail behind these bell-shaped creatures. The tentacles have strong protein-based venomous capsules (nematocysts) that can cause a severe allergic reaction. Along the southern Atlantic seaboard, the most common types of jellyfish are the box or cannonball varieties. The cannonball jellyfish causes very little, if any, discomfort. The box jellyfish and the Portuguese man-of-war will lay it on you with the most painful, agonizing sting imaginable.

If you are stung, wash off the attached tentacles using salt water. Avoid using fresh water, as it will worsen the painful inflammation. Apply vinegar if readily available. Remove any existing tentacles by scraping off with a knife or even a credit card. Applying urine to a jellyfish sting is not advised and will make the venomous cells swell, explode and cause more damage. Prompt medical evaluation is needed for severe stings, especially if they are causing serious symptoms affecting circulation or breathing.

Jellyfish and Portuguese man-of-wars are found all along the eastern seaboard. August is usually "jellyfish month" up and down the coastline. These translucent creatures resemble a slightly colored piece of plastic floating in the water. They are so much more! These invertebrates will gladly brush their tentacles against your extremities, causing excruciating pain. If you have the misfortune of a close encounter with one of these creatures, you will most likely require medical attention. The fastest remedy to give you relief is to apply vinegar to the sting, which helps neutralize the toxin. Higher-than-normal ocean temperatures have brought about an increase of jellyfish along the southeastern U.S. coast. Marine biologists blame the increase on several factors, including global warming and the overfishing of natural predators such as tuna.

Avoid stepping on a stingray by shuffling your feet through the sand as you wade into the surf. Rays scare easily and will flee when they are spooked. If you become impaled by one of these creatures, you are going to pray to Neptune for relief. After you get out of the water, clean the wound with soap and water. Soak the wound in hot water approximately 104 degrees Fahrenheit until the pain resolves. Carefully remove any barbs left from the stinger with pliers or tweezers. Again, seek medical attention as soon as possible. I strongly urge all surf fishermen to wear some fashion of aquatic sandal, such as Crocs or Keens, to eliminate this potential hazard.

Tight Lines, My Friends

Glossary

ARTIFICIAL REEFS: Man-made, underwater structures located offshore that attract marine life. These can include scrapped ships, old bridge structures, etc.

BAG LIMIT: Pertains to species that are regulated by law as to how many you may keep in a given day.

BAITFISH: Small fish caught and used as bait to attract larger fish.

BARBELS: The whisker-like sensory appendage on certain species of fish.

CARTILAGINOUS FISH: Species such as sharks and rays that do not have a spine or bone structure.

CAUDAL FIN: The tail fin of any fish.

CCA: Coastal Conservation Association.

CRUSTACEANS: Saltwater animals having no backbone, such as crabs, shrimp and lobster.

CUT BAIT: Fish or any other aquatic creature cut into chunks for bait.

DORSAL FIN: The large middle fin that runs along a fish's spine.

DRAG: The mechanical device on a reel that limits how fast the line can slip from the reel spool.

ECTOTHERMIC: Describes animals that control body temperature through external means.

ESTUARY: A protected backwater that provides shelter and food for juvenile fish to mature.

FERRULE UNION: The joint where different sections of a rod fit together.

GIG: An instrument for spearing fish.

ICHTHYOLOGIST: A scientist who studies fish.

IGFA: International Game Fish Association, based in Miami, Florida. This agency regulates fishing world records.

INTRACOASTAL WATERWAY (ICW): The Intracoastal Waterway is a combination of ocean bays and backwater canals that are used for passage for recreational boaters to travel up the eastern seaboard.

LATERAL LINE: The sensory organ on a fish that detects movement.

PECTORAL FIN: The fin located on each side of the body behind the gill opening.

PLANKTON: Microscopic plants and animals that drift in the water.

ROE: Fish eggs, considered a delicacy by some people.

SALINITY: The salt content of the water.

SHOAL: A submerged ridge or sandbar located off the shore.

SLOUGH: A depression that runs parallel to the beach, between the outer sandbar and the beach.

SWIM BLADDER: A gas-filled sac in the fish's body cavity that regulates buoyancy.

TRANSLUCENT: Transmittal of diffused light.

About the Author

When Cameron Wright was just a lad some forty years ago, his dad would take him fishing while on family beach vacations. Wright, a native Charlottean, has traveled the world and fished every continent on the globe. Cameron holds degrees from N.C. State University and Montreat College. He is a regularly featured commentator on ESPN. Cameron resides in Charlotte, North Carolina, with his wife, Liz, and three sons, Zach, Connor and Vance.

UPCOMING BOOK FROM AUTHOR AND HISTORIAN CAMERON WRIGHT
MY SOUTHERN SOUL

Patriots, pirates, rebels and redcoats long ago defined the South as our country's most historic region. Long before the American colonial period, our coastline bore witness to it all. Our few centuries of occupation have only afforded us a glimpse into the many secrets our shores do yield. Discover our rich inheritance that is an affirmation of our traditions and values, steeped in history.

Visit us at
www.historypress.net